TABBY PATTERNS

Classic (blotched) tabby

Mackerel (lined) tabby

Spotted tabby

Ticked tabby

Small & intermingled (European)

Larger & more defined (USA)

Calico (UK – Tortie & White)

Patched Tabby (UK – Tortie-tabby)

An Instant Guide to
CATS

A complete guide to pedigree cat breeds
described and illustrated in full color

DAVID BURN

ILLUSTRATED BY
CHRIS BELL

GRAMERCY BOOKS
NEW YORK

For Larraine

NOTE

In discussing cat breeds and varieties the use of some technical terms is unavoidable. If you encounter a word with which you are unfamiliar, you may find it explained in the introductory section on pages 8–13. Explanations of terms relating specifically to coat patterns and colors are given on pages 116–19. There is also an extensive glossary on pages 122–4.

This 2000 edition is published by Gramercy Books™,
an imprint of Random House Value Publishing, Inc.,
201 East 50th Street, New York, New York 10022.

Gramercy Books™ and colophon are trademarks of
Random House Value Publishing, Inc.

Random House
New York • Toronto • London • Sydney • Auckland
http://www.randomhouse.com/

Printed and bound in Malaysia

A CIP catalog record for this book is available
from the Library of Congress.

ISBN 0-517-12357-6
8 7 6 5 4 3 2

Contents

Introduction

Nearly a quarter of all households in North America and most European countries own a cat. There are more than 5 million in Britain and nearly 25 million in the United States. Even though only 1 in 15 or so is a member of a pedigree breed, there are nearly half a million pedigree cats in the UK alone. Sometimes, however, the visible distinction between pedigree and non-pedigree may be a small one; indeed, the only tangible difference might be that the former has the papers to prove its origins while the other does not. Depending on the often chance matings that produced them, some ordinary domestic cats, alley cats – call the non-pedigrees what you will – may well resemble an accepted breed. This book is therefore not just an aid to recognizing the purebreds themselves – though it certainly fulfills that purpose – it can also be used as a guide to the interesting exercise of trying to determine which of the breeds any cat-in-the-street most closely resembles.

How to use this book

The book is divided into four sections, color-coded in the band at the top of each page as follows:

---

1 Longhaired cats
Those with classically long, flowing coats (usually the longest among all cats). A single breed, the Persian (Long Hair) makes up this section.

---

2 Semi-longhaired cats
Breeds with long hair but usually not so long as that of cats in the first section. Some in fact may look quite short, especially in young animals or during the summer, but almost invariably the tail shows longer hair at all times.

---

3 Shorthaired cats
Breeds with obviously short hair overall, smooth and close-lying or evenly upstanding and velvety.

---

4 Unusual cats
Breeds of any coat length but with a clearly odd feature not shown by the majority of cats. This section includes tailless or very short-tailed breeds, those with folded ears, and those with unusual coats, including curly-, crinkly- or wavy-coated breeds and even a hairless one.

First establish that the cat you are concerned with does not belong to section 4 before trying to assign it to one of the other three sections. If it does belong to section 4, one of the following symbols in the heading band will enable you to locate the appropriate sub-section:

unusual
tail feature

unusual
ear feature

unusual
coat feature

If the cat falls within one of the first three sections the search can be narrowed further to a sub-section based on the shape of the head in combination with the ear size. Most breeds have a distinctive head conformation but in many cases the differences between them are not readily apparent to the untrained eye. Four types, however, are fairly easy to distinguish and when this feature is combined with ear sizes it is possible to assign a cat to one of the following groupings:

round head
short nose
small ears

round head
medium nose
small ears

round head
medium nose
medium ears

average head
medium nose
medium ears

average head
medium nose
large ears

wedge head
long nose
large ears

Assess the roundness of a head in face view and nose length in profile. In cats with long coats, or in stud males regardless of coat length, try to imagine what the shape of the head would be without the fur because long cheek hair can sometimes make an average head appear quite round. A round head is at least as broad as it is deep. A wedge head, on the other hand, is relatively narrow, elongate and clearly triangular in face view; the set of the large ears follows the line of the triangle, accentuating it. An "average" head is what you would imagine it to be, intermediate between round and wedge, and is the typical head shape of most ordinary domestic cats. Large ears on an average head are usually set more upright than they are on a wedge head. In profile round heads and average heads show a variably pronounced angle, or stop, between the nose and the forehead, whereas in wedge heads the profile is ideally straight, if not somewhat convex.

Using this system it should be possible to restrict your search to within a maximum of eight breeds, and in most cases four or fewer. Not all cats, however, fall neatly into this classification; some sit on or close to a division – several average-headed, large-eared cats, in particular, come close to having wedge heads (and vice-versa if they are not good examples of their breed). When this occurs search in the adjacent sub-section, in terms of both head shape and ear size (separately if needs be), as well.

9

Breeds and names

It is almost impossible to define the term "breed" because it means different things to different people. Perhaps the only attributes common to all breeds are that each has been accepted as such by some official organization somewhere, and that each possesses a combination of features that distinguishes it from other breeds recognized by the same organization. Because there is no universal agreement on what features should be included in that combination before a grouping can be considered distinct, breeds may be recognized at any level of difference. Hair length, for example, makes the otherwise identical Persian and Exotic separate breeds but in Britain the Exotic is considered to be a single breed, regardless of color or pattern, whereas the Persian (UK – Long Hair) is split into several breeds, some based on color alone, others based on pattern, regardless of color. In other cases the distinguishing feature may be the cat's type, a characteristic that is explained on page 12.

Different organizations, even within the same country, may use different criteria for classifying their cats. For example, all the cats that make up the single breed known as Balinese in Britain are divided into two breeds, Balinese and Javanese, in the USA. The use of different names by different organizations for the same grouping further adds to the confusion: the American Javanese, for example, is not the same breed as the one known by that name in Europe; but the European Javanese *is* the same breed as the UK Angora, which in America is known as the Oriental Longhair! Further complications arise because different organizations may not allow the same range of color varieties in a breed.

The book tries to tackle this confusion in several ways:
1. Except for the Burmese and Asian group cats, and one or two of the Oriental Short Hair group cats (see notes 3, 6 and 9 on pages 114–15), no grouping is regarded as a separate breed on the basis of color alone.
2. Breed/variety names used throughout are those recognized by the Cat Fanciers' Association (CFA) in the USA but if a breed is not recognized by the CFA, the name used is that recognized by the Governing Council of the Cat Fancy (GCCF) in the UK. The breed name in the main heading is in capital letters, followed by the variety name in lower case letters.
3. For breeds/varieties recognized by both the CFA and the GCCF the name used by the latter, which may or may not be the same name, is given beneath the main heading name. Alternative or outdated names in either country (which will be encountered in other books) may be shown in brackets on the appropriate line.
4. Names of breeds/varieties recognized by neither the CFA nor the GCCF are those that have the greatest currency in the literature. All such breeds are recognized by some official body somewhere but the CFA/GCCF standardization has been adopted here because they are the largest registering bodies in their respective countries. Other

such bodies exist in both these countries and elsewhere, most notably the *Fédération Internationale Féline* (FIFe) in Europe but lack of space precludes giving them full consideration. When breeds/varieties are shown as unrecognized in the USA and/or the UK it simply signifies that they are not yet recognized by the CFA and/or the GCCF respectively.

5. Though some recognition or nomenclature complications are covered on the breed pages themselves, others are discussed on pages 114–15 and can be accessed via the paw prints 🐾 at the foot of relevant breed pages.

Recognition

Before a grouping of cats that is claimed to be distinctive can be called a breed (or a new variety group or color variety within an existing breed) it must first be accepted by an official body. That body must be satisfied that the aspiring grouping has a large enough number of interested breeders to ensure adequate support and minimize in-breeding, and that it is bred to an agreed standard. This procedure is known as recognition and it proceeds in stages.

During the **preliminary** stage, which normally lasts for about five years in the USA and can be shorter or longer in the UK, the cats are shown in non competitive assessment classes where they are judged against their standard of points. This provides breeders with a means of monitoring how well their cats are progressing. Provided the registering organization is satisfied that the breed has sufficient support, merit and distinction it then moves to the stage of **provisional** recognition. By this time an official affiliated breed club will have been established and the standard of points may have been modified in the light of experience gained during the preliminary period. Throughout this provisional stage the cats may compete against each other in non-championship classes.

In the USA the provisional stage usually lasts for a year but in the UK it is generally two years (sometimes longer) before the breed has achieved sufficient show successes for it to be given **full** recognition. Not until a breed or variety has completed this process will it be eligible to be judged for championship status. The level of recognition that a breed has reached is frequently mentioned throughout this book; it can be an indication of how recently a breed has been developed and therefore how likely you are to encounter it.

Varieties

Most breeds show a range of varieties, some a very few (even only one) but others up to 200 or so. These are the product of the interaction of several genes responsible for the expression of color and pattern. Identifying an individual cat involves determining both its breed and its variety. Virtually all breeds of domestic cat that occur in the western world are represented in the book but clearly only a limited selection of varieties can be included for each of them. In those breeds represented here by more than one variety much of the text on a page may relate to the breed as a whole, so read through all the varieties to get a full picture of it. The genes responsible for color and pattern, and the varieties they produce, are explained on pages 116–19.

It is most important to understand that because nearly any coat color or pattern can be introduced into almost any breed, these most obvious features are unfortunately of little value in identifying the breed itself. In practice, however, most breeds show a limited range of varieties but there are many that do share at least some colors and patterns. Only where there is no overlap in the range may color or pattern be helpful in distinguishing a breed from others similar to it in other respects. The chart on pages 120–121 indicates the range of colors and patterns that you are likely to encounter in each breed. If you think you have identified a Blue Van Maine Coon Cat, for example, think again because the chart will tell you that the van pattern does not officially occur yet in that breed – but it does in the Norwegian Forest Cat, which is otherwise very similar.

The last text box on a page may contain details of breeds that could be confused with the one you think you have identified. Check these and eliminate them to confirm your identification. Use the index to do this as well; it contains many cross references not included elsewhere.

Types

The fundamental feature used in the classification of cat breeds is a characteristic known as type. This is the combined size, shape and proportions of the main parts of the body – head, ears, torso, legs and tail. Two extremes of type are recognized: the compact, sturdy, short-legged and broad, round-headed type exemplified by such breeds as the Persian and the British Shorthair; and the lithe, slender, long-legged and narrow, wedge-headed type that is typified by the Siamese. All examples of the former are generally referred to under the all-embracing term **cobby**. The extreme cobby cat is the Persian. The British call that breed the Long Hair but still use the term **Persian** to describe the type.

Because the cobby breeds historically developed in the western world, they (and those derived directly from them) are regarded as distinct from all the others, which are said to have **foreign** type. Though the original examples of the latter did develop in Asia, the term foreign, in itself, now carries no implication of place of origin. Within the foreign breeds those that tend towards the Siamese extreme are described as having **oriental** type.

Between the Persian and Siamese ends of the scale lies a range of various intermediate types. Some are unique to a breed; the type of

12

the Devon Rex, for example, is clearly oriental but in a form shown by no other breed. Others are shared by several breeds such as the distinctive, intermediate foreign type shown by the Burmese, Bombay, Burmilla and Tiffanie, whose individualities are based on other features such as coat length or color. It is not possible in this book to describe fully all the types that exist. The differences between some of them can appear quite subtle to the untrained eye but the range is reflected in the sub-section symbols shown on page 8. Examples of the basic types are illustrated on the front endpapers.

Type is frequently mentioned throughout the book but always remember that even within a breed there will be individual variation. Some cats are better examples than others, which may show less than classic type even though they have an equally high pedigree.

Specimen page

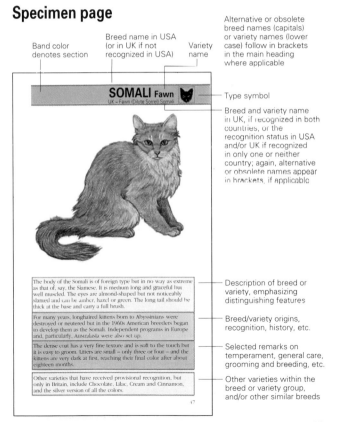

Band color denotes section

Breed name in USA (or in UK if not recognized in USA)

Variety name

Alternative or obsolete breed names (capitals) or variety names (lower case) follow in brackets in the main heading where applicable

SOMALI Fawn
UK – Fawn (Dilute Sorrel) Somali

Type symbol

Breed and variety name in UK, if recognized in both countries, or the recognition status in USA and/or UK if recognized in only one or neither country; again, alternative or obsolete names appear in brackets, if applicable

The body of the Somali is of foreign type but in no way as extreme as that of, say, the Siamese. It is medium long and graceful but well muscled. The eyes are almond-shaped but not noticeably slanted and can be amber, hazel or green. The long tail should be thick at the base and carry a full brush.

Description of breed or variety, emphasizing distinguishing features

For many years, longhaired kittens born to Abyssinians were destroyed or neutered but in the 1960s American breeders began to develop them as the Somali. Independent programs in Europe and, particularly, Australasia were also set up.

Breed/variety origins, recognition, history, etc.

The dense coat has a very fine texture and is soft to the touch but it is easy to groom. Litters are small – only three or four – and the kittens are very dark at first, reaching their final color after about eighteen months.

Selected remarks on temperament, general care, grooming and breeding, etc.

Other varieties that have received provisional recognition, but only in Britain, include Chocolate, Lilac, Cream and Cinnamon, and the silver version of all the colors.

Other varieties within the breed or variety group, and/or other similar breeds

47

This cat has the large, short-legged body and round, flat face that characterize the Persian. The coat is pure white with a silky texture. Blue-eyed, Orange-eyed and Odd-eyed (one blue, one orange) varieties exist. Green-eyed examples do occur but are not permitted in the standard. The tip of its nose is pink.

Developed from middle eastern cats first taken into Europe in the early 1500s. Victorian breeders blended the Persian type with the silky coat of blue-eyed Angoras from Turkey. The orange eye color derives from its Persian ancestry.

A placid but friendly cat, well suited to a calm, indoor life. By nature it spends a lot of time keeping itself clean but may need the owner's help with brown staining caused by skin oils. Many Blue-eyed Whites suffer from congenital deafness.

The Chinchilla is similar but has green eyes and black tipping on the fur. Turkish Angora, Maine Coon Cat and Norwegian Forest Cat have the same eye color varieties but are different in type.

A deep-bodied, short-legged cat of cobby appearance. As with all Persian type Long Hairs the head should be round and broad with full cheeks, a short nose and small ears set wide apart. The eyes are large and round, copper or deep orange in color, and the long, flowing coat is a lustrous raven black.

Originally called the Persian universally, and still known as that in the USA, this breed's name in the UK was changed to Long Hair many years ago. The Black was the first variety to be recognized officially in Britain and appeared at the first cat show in 1871.

Affectionate and reputedly more lively than the White Persian. Breeding the pure color is difficult but kittens with grayish-brown coats often attain a solid black at six months. Sunlight and damp conditions can turn the coat rusty.

The combination of color, body shape and head type distinguish it from all other longhaired cats. Black Smoke Persians, no matter how dark, always have paler shaded areas.

A large-bodied cat with the short legs and round head typical of the breed. The coat should be very long and an even shade throughout, with no trace of white hairs. The color is a blue-gray in various shades, though lighter forms are preferred. Kittens often show tabby markings which they outgrow.

This color probably originated from crossing Black Persians with Whites. Of all the Persian varieties the Blue comes closest to the perfect type and over the years it has been widely used for improving the breed and creating new varieties.

A gentle, friendly cat with a very even-natured disposition. In its early days, probably because Queen Victoria owned several, the Blue was extremely popular in "high society" and became very much a status symbol.

Blue solid-colored cats occur in several longhaired breeds but none has the luxuriance of coat of the true Persian. The flat face and small, wide-set ears also make it unmistakable.

The standard describes this color as a medium to dark chocolate, warm in tone and even in color, free from shading, markings or white hairs. The eye color is copper or deep orange. Body type is typically Persian – deep and cobby with a round, broad head, short nose and small ears set well apart.

This color, and the related lilac (following page), first appeared in the colorpoint program (see p.32). Because they carry Siamese blood they are classed as Himalayans in the USA, despite the eye color. In the UK they are simply colors of the Long Hair.

The only Siamese legacy that remains in this variety is the color and it now has the sedate but affectionate good nature that all Persian varieties possess. This, and its dilute version, the Lilac are the most uncommon members of the breed.

The only other cat of Persian type with which this one might be confused would be a poorly colored Black, some of which show a rustiness that gives them a brown look.

The use of Blues to improve the type of colorpoints produced some solid lilac kittens. These have been perfected in recent years to create this beautiful variety. The color, which is often referred to as lavender in America, is a warm, pinkish dove gray and, as in the Chocolate, should be free from any shading.

Genetically, lilac is a diluted chocolate. As these two are the only solid-colored cats to be derived from the colorpoint breeding program, they are sometimes distinguished by the name Kashmir in the USA.

Similar in temperament in all respects to its cousin, the Self Chocolate Himalayan. Breeding evenness of color into the coat is difficult and consequently good examples of this variety are still relatively rare. It is, however, fast gaining in popularity.

The lilac variety occurs in the longhaired Tiffanie and the Oriental Longhair breeds but in those the conformation is quite different. The head, in particular, of a true Persian is unmistakable.

With its rich orange coat and deep copper eyes, this is a most striking variety of the breed. Though inherent tabby markings are very difficult to mask they should not show through. The long, flowing coat can help to obscure them but they often persist on the head and it is rare to find perfect examples.

Though they first appeared as early as 1895, Solid Reds have never been common and loss of stock during the 1939–45 war depleted them further. A shortage of females (the red gene is sex-linked) is now being overcome as interest is revived.

The gene that suppresses the tabby coat in other solid colors is ineffective on red; creating a truly uniform color is therefore not possible – the tabby pattern can only be dissipated by careful selective breeding over a long period.

As with all members of the Persian breed, the general type of this variety makes it readily distinguishable from any of the solid reds that may be encountered in other longhaired cats.

The usual sturdy body and broad, flat face combine here with a color, once described as that of Devonshire cream, to produce a Persian of great distinction. In the USA a single shade of buff-cream is preferred but in Britain the shade may vary from pale to medium. The color should be even to the roots.

Probably descended from "fawn" Angoras (unrelated to the modern breed known in the UK by that name), the Cream was once regarded as an unwanted by-product of the British Red Self program. By the early 1900s it had become fashionable in its own right.

Cream is a dilute version of red but, being dilute, the genetically unavoidable tabby markings can be more readily masked. Kittens may show such markings but most should disappear within ten weeks. As in all Persians, litters tend to be small.

Could be confused with Red or Cream Cameo Persians but in those the color is restricted to the tips of the otherwise white hairs, rather than being even throughout the depth of the coat.

The ground color should be a rich, tawny sable bearing dense black, classic markings, the pattern of which, as with all tabbies, is precisely specified: this includes an M mark on the forehead, the shape of a butterfly on the shoulders, three parallel lines along the spine and an oyster mark on each flank.

Though popular when shows first began, tabbies have been rare in the UK since the 1920s but they are more numerous in the USA. As early as 1885, one aspiring owner offered $1000, over twenty times the usual price, for an outstanding example.

Careful, periodic outcrosses are needed to maintain the color and contrast of the pattern. Longhaired tabbies are usually groomed to make the coat lie flatter than in other varieties so that the markings can be seen more clearly.

This variety might be confused with the Chocolate Tabby Persian but that has rich brown markings on a bronze background. The mackerel pattern is also seen in the USA but not elsewhere.

The color in this variety is a random patchwork of black and orange/cream. The size of the patches is very variable, as is their distribution, which should be as even as possible. Ideally neither color should dominate. A pale blaze running from the top of the head down the nose is considered a desirable feature.

Thought not to have been one of the original Persian varieties imported from Asia, the Tortoiseshell probably arose from chance matings of Black Persians and shorthaired tortoiseshell non-pedigree cats. It was developed at the same time as the Solid Red.

As with all tortoiseshells this is a virtually all-female variety (the occasional males are almost invariably sterile). Consequently breeding for it is a hit-or-miss affair. On average, only half of the females from a Tortoiseshell will show their mother's coloring.

No other longhaired tortoiseshell has the large, cobby body type and round head that typify this breed. A version with chocolate replacing the black is provisionally recognized in the UK.

The Blue-Cream is a dilute version of the Tortoiseshell in which the black is replaced by blue and the red (orange) by cream. British examples have the colors subtly intermingled whereas the American standard requires that they should form distinct patches, neither one predominating.

This variety first appeared in the 1890s from solid Blue and Cream matings, designed to improve the type of Creams and to create paler Blues. Eventually the type quality of the Blue-Cream was appreciated and it was recognized in Britain in 1930.

Being a tortoiseshell, this is a female-only variety. The parent crosses that create it are considered to be very successful as they produce cats of excellent Persian type. It has an amenable temperament and is a good companion for people living alone.

It can resemble the Blue Persian but is distinctly variegated. Red tinged examples are considered imperfect. A Lilac-Cream version does have provisional recognition in Britain.

Often larger than other Persians, the Bi-color has patches of any solid color on white. The American standard expects the chest, underside, feet, legs and muzzle to be white, while that in the UK is less specific. A white inverted V running from the nose to the forehead is considered a desirable feature.

Full recognition of the Bi-color Persian came as late as the 1960s but the first standard, which required the markings to be symmetrical, was too demanding and it had to be revised. Since then numbers have increased rapidly.

The outcrossing involved in producing these cats ensures that they are robust and healthy. As with all the Persians, the coat must be well cared for and the white areas cleaned from time to time. Females are attentive to their kittens.

Black, Blue, Red and Cream versions are recognized in all countries. Britain allows Chocolate & White and Lilac & White as well. Tabby colors & White are also recognized.

In this variety white occurs with the tortoiseshell colors. The British standard requires a third to a half of the coat to be white, evenly distributed, but in America the cat is described as being white with colored patches, the white to predominate on the underbody and legs. Originally called the Chintz Cat in Britain.

The creation of a bi-colored version was one of the goals of the early Tortoiseshell breeders but it proved difficult to realize because little was then known of the sex-linked nature of the orange gene. Even now, maintaining a line requires much skill.

It was once said that the coat of this variety had a different texture to that of other Persians and was consequently easier to groom. Modern examples, however, seem little different from other varieties in this respect and should receive regular care.

The same color versions exist as in the Tortoiseshell but only the Calico and Dilute Calico (UK – Blue Tortie & White) are recognized in America.

The sparkling, metallic appearance of this most glamorous cat is caused by the presence of short, black tips on the otherwise pure white hairs of all regions except the underparts. The eyes, blue-green or emerald in color, are strikingly outlined in black. An extra-long ruff is considered a very desirable feature.

The first Chinchilla is thought to have appeared in a litter from a Silver Tabby in the late Victorian times. Early examples were different from those of today and tended to be darker, with various eye colors, and often bearing tabby markings.

More finely boned than other Persians, they are nonetheless just as robust and make lively, affectionate companions. Kittens often show tabby markings, which they usually outgrow. Frequently the darkest kittens turn into the palest adults.

The eye color and sparkling coat distinguish it from the White Persian. The only other single-color, shell-tipped Persians are the Red and Cream Cameos, which have deep orange eyes.

PERSIAN Shaded Silver
UK – Shaded Silver Long Hair

This is a black-tipped silver cat in which the tip length is longer than that of the Chinchilla. The dark shading on the face, down the back and on the top of the tail gradually dilutes to pure white on the underside but the outside of the legs is the same shade as the face. Darker overall than the Chinchilla Silver Persian.

Although this is an old variety, ever popular in America, it was dropped from full recognition in Britain in 1902 because it was difficult to distinguish from the early Chinchillas. Even now it is given only preliminary recognition in the UK.

Chinchillas and Shaded Silvers do occur in the same litter; both types of kitten look like dark tabbies at birth and the difference shows only as they grow. Correctly marked Shaded Silvers are more difficult to produce. Meticulous grooming is essential.

This variety could be confused with the Pewter Persian, which also has a black-shaded white coat. The Pewter's eye color, however, is orange or copper, not emerald green.

One of the silver group in which the pure white undercoat is tipped to a medium degree with color, heaviest on the mask, along the back, the top of the tail and the legs, lightest on the flanks, ruff and underparts. As with all tipped Persians the ruff should be extra long to show off the contrasting shades.

Cameos were created in the USA in 1954 from Tortoiseshell and Smoke crosses. The name is restricted in the UK to shell and shaded versions in Red, Cream and Tortoiseshell colors; in the USA it also includes red smokes and red-tipped tabbies.

Affectionate and very decorative, the Shaded Cameos have become very popular. They are healthy animals and generally exhibit good Persian type, perhaps because of their outcrossed background. Newborn kittens are almost white.

Distribution of the colored tipping varies between shaded and smoke cats. Shaded Cameos appear to be wearing a colored mantle, whereas Smokes have a much darker head and legs.

The colored tipping on the white coat of a Smoke Persian varies in length on different parts of the body: long, almost to the roots, on the back, head and feet, but shorter on the flanks and ruff. This produces a most beautiful cat with a contrasting ruff and a coat that seems to alter in shade as the animal moves.

First developed from Black, Blue and Silver crosses, and now maintained by occasional outcrosses to those varieties. Never numerous in Britain – almost extinct by 1945 – Smokes have always been popular in the USA where fine examples are bred.

Difficult to breed; kittens look solid-colored for many months. More difficult to groom than most longhairs. The coat is soon affected by damp and sunlight; many breeders say that it can be maintained in peak condition for only two months of the year.

Other Smoke Persians are Black, Blue, Cameo (UK – Red), Tortie and Blue-Cream (in USA and UK), and Lilac, Cream, Chocolate Tortie and Lilac Tortie (UK only).

29

PERSIAN Silver Tabby

UK – Silver Tabby Long Hair

The markings on this spectacular variety should be dense black on a silver (white with short, black tipping) background. The ruff should be silver and full. In Britain only the classic (blotched) pattern is accepted but in America the mackerel (lined) pattern is also recognized. The eyes can be green or hazel.

A rare cat, even today, but the Silver Tabby Long Hair has been seen at shows since they first began. The standard was often poor, however, and many animals had markings only on the legs and head. Modern examples are much improved.

Combining the full Persian type with the jet black and silver colors and the precise tabby pattern is very difficult. Breeders are commonly disappointed by the appearance of a brown tinge, or by poor contrast between pattern and background.

Other longhaired silver tabbies are found in the Oriental Longhair, Turkish Angora, Tiffanie, Maine Coon Cat and Norwegian Forest Cat breeds but none has the distinctive type of the Persian.

This cat has a standard tipped coat in which the underlying color is a warm cream to apricot. In theory the tipping can be in any of the basic colors but in most cats bred to date it is black. Shell versions are also possible but the distinction is not made in the UK standard and both are called shaded.

"Brownies," as they are affectionately known, have frequently occurred in Chinchilla breeding programs but have been ignored as a variety in their own right until very recently. A wider range of colors than presently exists can be expected.

The Golden is an emergent variety and relatively few exist but there is no reason to suppose that they will be any different in temperament to other Persians – aristocratic in bearing, calm, affectionate and sociable, even with other cats.

Though superficially a red cat, it is easily distinguished from Cameos and Red Smokes by its green eyes. The shell-tipped version is sometimes known as a Golden Chinchilla.

Himalayans (UK – Colorpoints) combine the long coat and Persian body type with the colors and markings of the Siamese breed. The points (mask, ears, tail and legs/feet) carry the named color, which is sharply contrasted with a paler, complementary body color. As in the Siamese cat, the eye color must be blue.

After several failed attempts to create this combination, started in the early 1920s, success came in the mid-1950s when the variety was given recognition on both sides of the Atlantic. Progress was helped by work on cat genetics at Harvard.

Himalayans have inherited only the coloring of their oriental forebears, not the extrovert temperament, and they show all the characteristic calm of the Persian. As with all cats of Persian type litters are small, two or three kittens being the usual.

The Himalayan range includes all the standard colors and the points can be tabby or tortie patterned. Other longhaired breeds with Siamese markings are the Balinese, Birman and Ragdoll.

Distinct tabby markings show on the point areas and include an M mark on the forehead, broken rings on the front legs and tail, and barring on the front of the hind legs. In this colored variety the body color is a glacial white; in the others it tends to a hue that reflects the point color.

Developing the Himalayan group took a long time because it is very difficult to fix the classic Persian type in cats with the required coat pattern. Simply crossing Persian and Siamese yields only shorthaired, solid-colored kittens.

A young adult Himalayan's body color may darken when the coat gets longer after it sheds for the second time. Kittens are born a uniform cream-white; the point colors begin to show in a few days but may take over a year to reach full intensity.

The Balinese is perhaps the most superficially similar breed but its fur is shorter and it is of obvious Siamese type, any tendency towards which is a serious fault in Persian type Himalayans.

A variety that conforms in all respects to the Persian type except in the face. The nose is very short, often depressed into an indentation between the eyes, which are very prominent. A furrow runs down the back of the muzzle from the inside of the eye to the corner of the mouth.

It occurs as a spontaneous mutation in litters of Solid Red and Red Tabby Persians. The Peke-Face enjoys considerable popularity in the United States but has consistently been denied recognition in Britain on health grounds.

Breeders must show restraint in not exaggerating the deformity too much as it can cause breathing problems. Other difficulties can include poor opposition of upper and lower teeth and, because of the wrinkled muzzle, blockage of the tear ducts.

The only Peke-Face varieties are Solid Red and Red Tabby. As the full facial characteristics do not show in kittens for several months, confusion at that age with normal examples is possible.

The Birman is an exclusively colorpointed breed whose distinctive feature is its white boots. The body is large but less cobby and longer than that of a Persian, and the fur is not so full. American examples tend to have a more pronounced ruff than those bred in Britain.

Though the true origins remain a mystery, legend has it that centuries ago these cats were guardians of a temple in Burma. In 1919 a pregnant female was sent from Indochina to France where the breed was developed and then recognized in 1925.

The combination of its handsome appearance and its intelligent, affectionate, playful nature makes the Birman one of the most popular of all pedigree cats. It matures early and can breed in the first year. The litter size is usually three to five.

In appearance it is difficult to distinguish between this breed and the Mitted Ragdoll but the latter is more heavily built, has a slightly longer tail and its eyes are somewhat more slanted.

The head shape of the Birman is intermediate between that of the Persian and the Balinese – fairly broad and round but with a medium length nose. In the Blue Point the body color is a cold, bluish-white with blue-gray points, darker in American examples. Birman eye color is blue – the deeper the better.

Although it was almost wiped out in World War II the French stock revived and a breeding nucleus was imported to Britain in the 1960s. The breed was established in America from a pair of Tibetan temple kittens sent there in 1960.

Females in season can be rather restless and they mate with enthusiasm. They are attentive, responsible mothers to their kittens, which average four to a litter. As with all longhaired cats Birmans should be groomed regularly but the fur does not mat.

As well as Seal and Blue Points, Lilac and Chocolate are also recognized in the USA; all these, along with tabby, tortie and tortie-tabby points, have full recognition in the UK.

The Ragdoll is a large, stocky colorpointed breed, similar in appearance to the Birman but generally heavier and with thicker fur. Its chief characteristic, however, is its remarkably placid temperament. When picked up it is said to relax to the point of limpness and hangs on the arm like a ragdoll – hence its name.

The origin of this breed is a subject of controversy. Claims have been made that it derives from a single cat (in the USA) whose extreme passivity was acquired from the shock of being involved in a road accident and was then inherited by her offspring.

Along with its reputation for docility, this cat was also said to be insensitive to pain (but this has been disproved) and to lack fear (but so do many cats). Do not rely on every one you meet living up to its image – some can be just as lively as any other cat!

The basic colorpoint variety occurs in three pattern versions: plain, as here, mitted (with white boots) and bi-colored, in which specified areas of white can be present.

37

In the typical Ragdoll the head is large, with full cheeks and a rounded muzzle. The nose is of medium length and has only a slight break in its profile. The mitted variety has white boots and white on the underside from chin to belly. A narrow white blaze on the nose is also permitted.

The "road accident" theory of the breed's origin can safely be dismissed on the grounds of genetic impossibility. It is far more likely to have been developed by selective breeding from a litter that spontaneously showed the extreme docile temperament.

The breed's lack of fear is accompanied by an unwillingness to fight. Together, these make it extremely vulnerable to other cats, dogs and even boisterous children. It is very tolerant and makes a faithful and devoted pet, well suited to indoor living.

This is variety that most closely resembles the Birman but is stockier, has denser fur, slightly smaller, more almond-shaped eyes and, of course, a totally different temperament.

The bi-color variety is an extension of the mitted variety, the variable gene for white-spotting achieving fuller expression. White should be present on the bib, chest, underbody and the front legs overall. A white inverted V extending down the nose and over the muzzle to the chin is an important feature.

Despite the mystery and lack of documentation surrounding its origins, the breed is known to have appeared in California in the 1960s. Its temperament appeals to many people and it now has preliminary recognition on both sides of the Atlantic.

Newborn kittens are almost white, taking perhaps two to three years to reach their full color. The fur, which "breaks" as the cat moves, is said to need little attention; it is noticeably shorter in the summer months than in winter.

Bi-colored colorpointed cats occur in only one other breed, the Oriental Longhair – the American version of the UK Angora in which colorpoint varieties are not accepted (see p.54).

This is essentially a Burmese cat with long hair. It has a foreign body type but not so extreme as that of the Siamese. The head is like that of the Burmese and the eyes are golden yellow. The tail fur is longer than body fur and there is a distinct ruff around the neck. The variety illustrated is the Burmese version of black.

Developed in the UK (together with the Burmilla and other shorthaired cats in the Asian group) by selective breeding from the results of an accidental mating between a Burmese and a Chinchilla in 1981. It received preliminary recognition in 1990.

Gentleness and an even temperament are high on the list of characteristics that Tiffanie breeders are aiming to fix in their cats. The coat is fine and silky and, as in most semi-longhairs, its color and length develop slowly.

Most colors (and their Burmese versions) and patterns are accepted except bi-color and colorpoint. A daintier cat than either the Maine Coon Cat or the Norwegian Forest Cat.

The Maine Coon Cat is a large, muscular cat of rugged appearance. The coat is heavy, shorter on the forequarters but lengthening along the back and down the flanks, and shaggy on the belly and breeches. Despite its bulk the fur is silky to the touch. The tail is long with plume-like, not bushy, fur.

One of the oldest natural North American breeds, believed to have derived from longhaired cats, possibly original Angoras, brought to the state of Maine by seamen in the 1850s, which bred with resident shorthairs to create a range of varieties.

Maine Coon Cats make excellent house pets. They are affectionate, playful and intelligent. The coat is relatively easy to groom but should be combed weekly to avoid knotting, particularly of the longer chest and belly fur. They are avid hunters.

The variety range includes all color and pattern combinations except chocolate, lilac, and colorpoint. Some non-pedigree semi-longhaired cats superficially resemble this breed.

This is the commonest variety. The color and pattern of the coat is reminiscent of that of a Racoon, hence the name that was given to the breed. Maine Coon eye colors are shades of green, gold or copper (also blue and odd in Whites); any combination of eye and coat color is permissible.

Maine Coon Cats were very popular in America at the turn of the century but as show cats they lost favor when Persians began to be imported from Britain. Interest revived in the 1950s and the breed was eventually recognized by the CFA in 1967.

Although a large breed it may take as long as four years to reach full size. Despite its docile and home-loving nature it is hardy and can withstand a fair degree of discomfort. Cold winters present no problem and it will sleep in the most unlikely places.

Distinguishing a Maine Coon Cat from a Norwegian Forest Cat is not easy but it has a broader muzzle, slightly more dished profile and its ears are a little more widely set.

Bi-colored versions of all the colors and patterns, including tortie and blue-cream are common in this breed. The American standard requires a third of the body to be white; the British standard is less precise but both are agreed that white must show on the bib, belly and feet.

After their revival in the USA a number of Maine Coons were sent to Europe, notably to Germany, where they quickly found favor. American stock was imported to Britain in 1983 and the breed was given full recognition by the GCCF in 1994.

Litters are quite small, two or three kittens being the usual and rarely exceeding four. They mature relatively slowly. Because the Maine Coon's genetic background is so varied each kitten in a litter may be a different color/pattern combination.

Turkish Angoras may seem similar but they are smaller, of more foreign type with almond-shaped, slanting eyes and finer, silkier fur that has a tendency to wave and lacks a woolly undercoat.

This is a natural breed, native to Scandinavia. Centuries of living outdoors in the harsh climate have produced an exceptionally rugged, strong cat with a thick, weatherproof coat. The head is broadly triangular with a medium length, straight nose. The ears are set wide apart and sometimes bear pronounced tufts.

Its true origins are unknown but it may well be the cat of Norse mythology and is probably the "fairy cat" of fables written in the early 1800s. First tamed by farmers, it caught the attention of breeders in the 1930s and a pedigree was developed.

The breed has an independent nature but it is playful and does enjoy human company. It much appreciates free access to the outdoors. It has strongly developed claws that it uses to good effect in climbing and hunting.

All combinations of color and pattern except chocolate, lilac, and colorpoint are possible. Some semi-longhaired non-pedigree cats superficially resemble this breed.

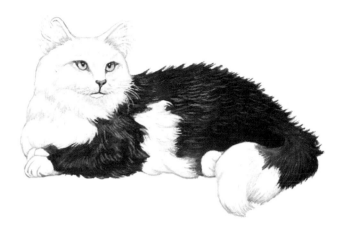

Bi-colored and tri-colored varieties can show any amount of white. Norwegian Forest Cats are strongly built with a solid bone structure. The legs are stocky, longer at the back, and the feet large. The density of the coat varies with the season, reaching full proportions only in the winter months.

Not until the 1970s did the the breed attract much attention outside Scandinavia. It was recognized by the FIFe in 1983 but as yet has only preliminary recognition in Britain. After a six-year probation it gained full CFA recognition in 1994.

Though the water-repellent coat is thick, it requires surprisingly little attention. Like all cats, it sheds in the late spring, and throughout the summer it appears to be relatively short-haired, lacking the woolly undercoat – only the tail fur remains long.

The Norwegian Forest Cat strongly resembles the Maine Coon Cat but it tends to have a bushier tail, more pointed muzzle, slightly more slanted eyes and a narrower space between the ears.

SOMALI Ruddy
UK – Usual (Black) Somali

The Somali is basically a longhaired Abyssinian and as such carries the handsome agouti (ticked) coat of its parent breed. A short vertical line rising above each eye is all that remains of the fundamental tabby pattern. A lynx-like tuft of hair at the tip of the large ears is desirable but not always present.

Originally thought to be a spontaneous mutation, the Somali is now believed to derive from some non-pedigree Abyssinians that carried the recessive gene for long hair and were registered in Britain in the 1930s.

It may be cautious at first, but once it feels secure the Somali is an affectionate, playful companion. Its wild appearance belies its home-loving nature, though it does need to spend time outdoors. It seems not to contend with cold weather very willingly.

The other semi-longhair in which the ticked tabby coat may be seen, but rarely, is the Oriental Longhair. Red (UK – Sorrell), Blue and Fawn are the breed's other universally recognized colors.

The body of the Somali is of foreign type but in no way as extreme as that of, say, the Siamese. It is medium long and graceful but well muscled. The eyes are almond-shaped but not noticeably slanted and can be amber, hazel or green. The long tail should be thick at the base and carry a full brush.

For many years, longhaired kittens born to Abyssinians were destroyed or neutered but in the 1960s American breeders began to develop them as the Somali. Independent programs in Europe and, particularly, Australia were also set up.

The dense coat has a very fine texture and is soft to the touch but it is easy to groom. Litters are small – only three or four – and the kittens are very dark at first, reaching their final color after about eighteen months.

Other varieties that have received provisional recognition, but only in Britain, include Chocolate, Lilac, Cream and Cinnamon, and the silver version of all the colors.

47

This is a medium-sized breed, light-boned and long in the body and leg. The wide head tapers towards the chin and bears high set, upright ears. The almond-shaped eyes slant slightly. These characteristics combine with a very fine and soft, silky coat (which lacks a woolly undercoat) to give a most elegant animal.

Beginning in 1962 this breed was established in the USA using cats from the Ankara Zoo in Turkey. Its followers like to think of it as a revival of the original Angora, whose identity in the west was lost by crossing it with Persians in the late 1800s.

The Turkish Angora has a gentle, well-behaved disposition but is energetic at play. When the cat is on the move the long tail is carried horizontally over the body. An ideal house cat, it has a reputation for sitting motionless, sphynx-like, for long periods.

Some purists consider that the White Turkish Angora is the only true representative of the breed but a wide range of varieties exists. The UK Angora is a different, more oriental breed.

Known simply as the Turkish when first recognized in the UK, this cat is like the Turkish Angora but is more robust. Eye color can be blue, amber or odd. The distribution of the color (cream or auburn), which may show tabby markings, is characteristic. This so-called van pattern occurs in very few other breeds.

This breed was nurtured in Britain, starting with a pair obtained from the Lake Van region of Turkey in 1955. In its homeland it probably evolved naturally from the very similar Turkish Angora, the other native breed, as a result of geographical isolation.

This breed's unusual willingness to enter water, and even swim, is well known; giving it a bath is relatively easy. The soft, silky fur, which lacks a woolly undercoat, reaches full expression only in the winter; the cat can resemble a shorthair in the summer.

Only the Amber-eyed Auburn has full recognition in the UK (the others are preliminary). Black, Blue and torties also occur in the USA. The van pattern may also be seen in the Norwegian Forest Cat.

The Balinese is thought to be a natural, longhaired mutation of the Siamese. Only colorpoint varieties occur. Its has a slender body, like the parent breed, and a fairly narrow, tapering head, though often slightly less so than in the Siamese. The flat-lying, silky coat is shorter than that of Himalayan Persians.

In the1950s some fluffy kittens appeared in litters of American pure-bred Siamese. Initially regarded as freaks, they bred true and were eventually developed as a separate breed. It was introduced into the UK in 1974 and is now fully recognized there.

Its graceful movement reminded early breeders of Balinese dancers. Apart from that it has no connection with the island of Bali from which its name is derived. It is lithe and acrobatic, sociable and affectionate but has a loud, compelling voice.

The only colorpointed longhaired cat with a long head. Points can be any color and can show tabby/tortie markings, but only plain seal, blue, chocolate and lilac are recognized in the USA.

This color variety has pinkish-gray points on an even, glacial white body. The body color of the Blue Point is similar and that of the Chocolate Point is ivory. As in all Balinese the eyes are a clear, vivid blue and are somewhat almond-shaped, slanting slightly downwards towards the nose.

Early Siamese cats were heavier bodied and the head was shorter than those of today. These features tend to persist in some Balinese but British breeders in particular try to bring them closer to the modern type by periodic cross-breeding.

Because the Balinese fur has no downy undercoat it is silkier, lies flatter and is less prone to matting than that of the Long Hair. The queens mature early, make excellent mothers and bear, on average, three or four kittens in a litter.

Balinese with less than the classic oriental head shape can be distinguished from plain Ragdolls by the much more lean body, and from Mitted Ragdolls and Birmans by the lack of white feet.

JAVANESE Seal Lynx Point
UK – Seal Tabby Point Balinese

This is one of a range of varieties within the Balinese in which tabby markings show up on the points in the form of banding on the legs and tail, and stripes around the eyes and on the nose and forehead. On the paler color varieties the pattern may be fairly indistinct but the M mark on the head is always visible.

After a 10-year development the Balinese was recognized in the USA in 1963. It is, however, restricted there to the four classic Siamese point colors. The other colors and patterned points were later recognized but as a separate breed, the Javanese.

Like that of the Siamese, the body color of most Balinese/Javanese has a tendency to darken as the cat grows older. Nonetheless a fairly clear contrast between points and background should remain visible, even in the paler colored varieties

The full range of marked points can exist – tabby, tortie and tortie-tabby – in all colors, but only in Britain are these included within the Balinese breed; in the USA they are all Javanese.

This is the longhaired version of the Oriental Shorthair or, to put it another way, the non-colorpoint version of the Balinese. It shows the extreme foreign type of the Siamese with a long, tubular body, long, slender legs and a long, tapering head whose triangularity is accentuated by the wide and outward set of the large ears.

The breed was created in Britain in the early 1970s using cats that appeared among the descendants of a mating between a Siamese and an Abyssinian that must have been carrying the long hair gene. It has preliminary recognition from the GCCF.

Oriental Longhairs are friendly, talkative cats that become very attached to their owners but readily allow others into their territory. They are gracefully athletic and playful. Their gentle and trusting nature makes periodic brushing a straightforward task.

Turkish Angora, Maine Coon Cat and Norwegian Forest Cat are other semi-longhaired breeds that may be similarly colored and/or patterned but this one is much more obviously oriental in type.

A fine, silky, coat and plume-like tail are hallmarks of the breed. There is no undercoat and the fur is close-lying. Eye color is green (blue and odd blue/green in the White); this contrasts with the Turkish Angora, which usually has amber eyes but they can be green in the Silver Tabby.

This is one of the newest breeds to be recognized in America. It was created there independently of the British program using Colorpoint and Oriental Shorthairs, Balinese, Javanese and Siamese and was accepted for registration by the CFA in 1988.

Litters average four but can be larger and the kittens open their eyes and begin play fights much earlier than is usual. The full coat is not developed until the cat is two years old. It sheds heavily for the summer, becoming virtually shorthaired.

Virtually all colors and patterns are allowed. Colorpointed examples occur only in the US where they must be bi-colored with white to distinguish them from Balinese/Javanese.

This is the short-haired version of the Persian and should conform to that breed's standard in all respects except coat length. The large, cobby body sits low on short, thick legs, and the head is large and round with a snub nose and small ears set wide and low. The eyes are large and round.

A product of selective breeding in the USA during the 1960s by crossing American Shorthairs and Persians. The aim was to create a cat of Persian beauty and tranquility but with a coat that was much easier to maintain.

The Exotic makes a good companion cat, loyal and affectionate but not demanding, and it can be somewhat more playful than its longhaired ancestors. Like many hybrids it is a hardy and healthy animal that presents few problems to its owner.

All colors, patterns and combinations are permitted, ranging from solid-colored through tipped (silver and golden) to van pattern and colorpointed. Tabbies can be classic, mackerel or spotted.

EXOTIC SHORTHAIR Black Smoke
UK – Black Smoke Exotic

The coat of the Exotic is slightly longer than that of other short-haired cats but its chief characteristic is that it has retained the long down hairs of the Persian, giving it a unique fullness. The plush, springy feel and chubby look have earned for the Exotic the nickname of "Teddy-bear cat".

The breed was given full recognition in America in 1967, since when it has competed with great success against breeds of much longer standing. Not yet numerous in Britain, where it has provisional recognition, it is, however, gaining in popularity.

One reason for the relative scarcity of this breed is that about half of all kittens born are longhaired because it is constantly being bred back to Persians to retain and improve type. Four is the usual litter size, as with most shorthairs.

Animals that show less than the ideal type may approach the look of chunkier examples of the British Shorthair. The latter, however, never achieve the fullness of coat of the Exotic.

Evenness in length of the Exotic's coat is important; there should be no tufting in the ears or between the toes, and no suggestion of a ruff. The eye color of pointed varieties (and one of the Whites) is a clear blue. Black tipped varieties have green eyes; all others have orange or gold eyes.

Some early Exotics carried Burmese blood, introduced in an attempt to improve type (American Burmese are cobbier than their UK cousins), but it had an unwanted effect on the color range and was subsequently excluded from the pedigree.

The thick fur has a natural tendency to stand rather than lie close to the body as it does in other shorthairs. This should be acknowledged during the occasional grooming sessions that might be required.

Discounting Rex cats, other shorthaired breeds that can be colorpointed are the Siamese (at the opposite end of the type spectrum!) and the British Shorthair.

The British Shorthair is of classic cobby type: the body is short and deep, with broad shoulders and rump, set on short, sturdy legs; the head is round, with full cheeks and a medium to short length nose. Of all the solid-color varieties, the Blue is usually regarded as coming closest to the perfect type.

This breed can be regarded as the native cat of Britain and is descended from cats introduced into northern Europe by the Romans 2000 years ago. Periodic crossing with cats of Persian type has produced the round-headed, cobby version of today.

Because of its long, self-sufficient history the British Shorthair is a hardy breed, well suited to coping with adverse conditions. The fact that it has had to contend with all kinds of hardship has given it much strength of character and a healthy constitution.

It is bred in all solid colors but in continental Europe the blue variety is judged by a slightly different standard and in France and the US is considered to be a separate breed, the Chartreux (p.64).

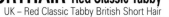

Clearly defined markings are the hallmark of a good tabby. Most non-pedigree tabbies show poor contrast between the dark and pale areas. In all members of the breed the ears are relatively small (but not so small as in the Exotic), and the eyes are large and round, set well apart.

The breed was developed in the 19th century from the best examples of native street and farm cats. The medium-height, stocky type used as a foundation had arisen naturally from its lean, leggy forebears of medieval times.

All British Shorthairs are good-natured, affectionate and intelligent – all qualities that make them ideal, undemanding household pets. They have a gentle voice and by-and-large are well behaved and untemperamental.

Classic, mackerel and spotted tabby patterns occur in all colors. British Shorthairs, in general, are cobbier and have a more rounded head than American Shorthairs.

BRITISH SHORTHAIR Tortoiseshell
UK – Tortoiseshell British Short Hair

The coat in British Shorthairs is described as being short, dense and firm to the touch; fluffiness is a fault. The colors in Tortoiseshells should be evenly intermingled but each one clearly defined. They should not form patches but a short, narrow blaze on the face is allowed.

In the early days of the pedigree cat the British Shorthair was the dominant breed but by the end of the 19th century Persians outnumbered it on the show bench by four to one. Since then it has recovered only slightly in relative popularity.

Well marked Tortoiseshells are difficult to breed, partly because, being an all-female variety, they must be mated to solid-color males (usually Blacks, Reds or Creams). Litters contain a mix of colors that may not include even one Tortoiseshell.

There is also a Blue-Cream (dilute tortoiseshell) variety. Lilac Tortie and Chocolate Tortie also have preliminary recognition in Britain but not in America.

The UK standard for bi-color varieties used to require the markings to be like those of a Dutch rabbit and symmetry was all-important. This proved to be too demanding and in 1971 it was changed to allow a more random pattern provided that white was restricted to between a third and a half of the body.

In continental Europe the breed is known as the European Shorthair. Most varieties are judged there by standards almost identical to the British and much of the present continental stock has some British ancestry.

All members of this breed are avid hunters of small mammals and birds. They will hunt, seemingly for pure enjoyment, even when they are not hungry and often play endlessly with their hapless victims.

Bi-colors can occur in any color; tabbies and tortoiseshells can also have white markings. British Shorthairs have longer noses, larger ears and are less cobby than Exotics.

In Smoke varieties the colored tipping on the guard hairs should contrast strongly with the white base color. This gives the cat a flickering appearance when it moves. Good Creams are rare because the tabbiness inherent in all cats is difficult to mask in the red-derived colors and faint markings often show.

Though they were imported into America early in their history, British Shorthairs received little attention from breeders there and remained rare for many years. A revival of interest led to their full recognition in 1980, but in a limited range of varieties.

Affection, food and shelter are all that the British Shorthair requires of its owner. It can care for its own coat perfectly well, though, as with all shorthairs, an occasional brushing can be beneficial, especially when it is shedding.

Only Black and Blue Smokes are recognized in the USA but in Britain the smoke coat is allowed in any of the standard colors and their tortoiseshell combinations.

A striking black pattern combines here with a tipped white ground color to give one of the most beautiful of all the varieties. British Shorthairs as a whole can be thought of as intermediate in appearance between the Exotic and American Shorthairs; most other shorthairs are more foreign in type.

A shortage of stud males after World War II forced breeders to use other shorthairs of foreign body type, with a resultant loss of the British Shorthair's heavy conformation. Careful crossing with Blue Persians in the 1950s has restored this.

Whatever the variety, this is an ideal family breed. It gets on well with children and may even befriend the family dog. Females kitten with little difficulty. The average litter size is four and the kittens develop quickly, becoming mobile in about a month.

The spotted tabby pattern can be in any color (except lilac and chocolate in the USA) and can occur in either the standard or the silver variety groups.

A native of France, this breed has a sturdy body, strong bones, solid muscles and a somewhat rounded head. The thick coat, which can be in any shade of blue, has a slightly woolly texture. The eyes are gold to copper, the deeper and more orange the better. It is described as having a sweet, smiling expression.

Said to be derived from cats bred by French monks in the 16th century. Outcrossing to Persians and British Shorthairs to save it from extinction after the war resulted in loss of type but the US breed is based solely on original French stock.

Despite its robust build the Chartreux is very agile and plays with much enthusiasm but is very gentle, males in particular. It has several dog-like qualities: it will retrieve, come to the call of its name and is very devoted to its owner.

Regarded by many as identical to the Blue British Shorthair but the true Chartreux (by the US standard) has a less rounded head and can be any shade from ash to slate. (See also p.78.)

This is a lithe but muscular cat with a sleek coat, and a thinnish tail of medium length. US and UK standards for the head differ, Americans preferring a more rounded and somewhat shorter-faced cat than the British. Sable (genetically a modified black) is regarded by some as the only true color for the breed.

This was the first pedigree breed to be developed in America. It derives from a single female taken there from Burma in 1930. At first a Siamese stud was used and the offspring back-crossed to the mother. Over several generations the breed was fixed.

The Burmese is a highly intelligent breed that loves people. Its gymnastics (it has been described as an animated pogo-stick) have given it quite a reputation as an entertainer. It will readily adapt to town or country conditions.

The coloring of the Sable is distinctive – blacker than in the Havana Brown, and more even than in the darkest of Natural Mink Tonkinese (both of which have green, not yellow, eyes).

The Champagne, and its dilute form, Platinum (UK – Lilac), were first bred in America in the 1960s. They were then classed, along with the Blue, as a separate breed, the Malayan, but the CFA now accepts them as Burmese. Coloring in most varieties is slightly shaded, becoming paler on the underside.

The breed was recognized by the CFA in 1936 but suspended in 1947–53 because the standard was being compromised by too much crossing with Siamese. More cats were imported from Burma to avoid this and to reduce inbreeding.

Burmese require little special attention. They enjoy a vigorous brushing, which strips out loose hair and maintains the glossy look. They get on well with each other and many an owner has reaped double enjoyment from having two rather than one.

In paler Burmese the color tends to be slightly darker on the points, particularly the ears and mask. This is also the case in Tonkinese (which have blue-green eyes), but more noticeably.

In the 1970s British breeders developed Red, Cream and four Tortoiseshell varieties of the Burmese. The GCCF regards these as varieties but the CFA recognizes them as a separate breed, Foreign Burmese. The tortoiseshell colors (brown, blue, chocolate and lilac) are generally paler than in other breeds and form a smaller pattern.

Some original Sable Burmese were exported from the USA to Britain in the late '40s and recognized by the GCCF in 1952. The Blue variety was developed in the UK soon after and gained recognition in 1960.

Females mature early and are very productive; the average litter is five but can be as many as ten. Kittens are very active: one American breeder has likened raising a litter to making popcorn! It is a long-lived breed, often reaching 18 years or more.

A glossy, close-lying coat, slightly rounded head, ears that are definitely at the larger end of the medium scale, and distinctive color range separate the Burmese from most other breeds.

BOMBAY
UK – Bombay

A jet black, close-lying coat, described as having a shimmering patent leather sheen, and the Burmese head and body type characterize this medium-sized, man-made breed. Combined with the large, round, widely set eyes, which are gold to vivid copper, these give the Bombay an unmistakable look.

Starting in 1958 an American breeder set out to create a black panther in miniature by crossing a Black American Shorthair with a Sable Burmese. In 1976 the resulting Bombay was recognized by the CFA. It has preliminary recognition in the UK.

This breed is affectionate and playful, very agile and seems to enjoy human company. In many respects its personality is dog-like: it can be readily trained to the leash, is a good retriever and guards its territory. It is an ideal indoor cat.

As yet there are no other varieties. The only other breed of remotely similar type that has a solid black is the American Shorthair but coat texture and head shape distinguish it.

Essentially a tipped (shell or shaded) Burmese, with the base coat in standard colors or silver (white). The tipping is densest along the spine and down the tail, dispersing down the flanks. Faint tabby markings show on the head, legs and tail. An outline of color accentuating the eyes is an important feature.

A relatively new breed, developed in the UK from the results of an accidental cross in 1981 between a Chinchilla Long Hair and a Lilac Burmese. It has its own breed club, formed in 1985, and was given provisional recognition by the GCCF in 1994.

This most beautiful and distinguished looking cat is fast gaining in popularity but as yet its numbers are low. Some have been introduced into North America. In temperament it is said to be affectionate, even-tempered and unassuming.

Varieties can be in any color (except cinnamon and fawn) or their tortie versions. The Burmese type separates it from tipped varieties of British, American, Oriental and Exotic Shorthairs.

Intermediate in type between the Burmese and Siamese in virtually all respects, this breed has colored points that are indistinctly defined against a body color that is only slightly paler and which itself is intermediate between the equivalent Burmese and Siamese colors. Eyes green-blue to light blue.

This is a hybrid of the Siamese and Burmese, developed in its own right in Canada from the late 1960s and recognized by the CFA in 1984. In the UK it has preliminary recognition in all the Burmese colors, and in their tabby and tortie-tabby versions.

A Tonk is full of character. It is very active, finds it hard to keep its inquisitiveness in check and much enjoys human company. It will respond to discipline but perhaps the best way of keeping it from looking for trouble is to provide it with a companion.

The other American varieties are Champagne Mink (chocolate), Blue Mink and Platinum Mink (lilac). The "low contrast" colorpoint pattern is characteristic of this breed (but see p.66).

In type, the American Shorthair is characterised by a total lack of any shorthair extremes. It is even more of an intermediate between the Exotic, at one end of the scale, and the Oriental Shorthair, at the other, than is the British (which it does, however, resemble). Most colors/patterns, except colorpoint, exist.

As North America is known not to have had any indigenous domestic cats, this breed is considered to be descended from animals taken to America by 17th century settlers from Europe. These quickly established themselves in large numbers.

As the American standard for this breed puts it "no part of the anatomy is so exaggerated as to foster weakness." It is ideally structured for its original role as a hardy, self-sufficient, working cat, capable of thriving in most conditions.

The other solid colors are white, black, blue and cream. The breed as a whole may be confused with the British Shorthair but it has a longer body and a less rounded, longer-nosed head.

The head of the American Short Hair is large and full-cheeked, slightly more triangular than round in face view, and with a squarish, medium length muzzle. The ears are a little larger than in the British Short Hair. The body is medium to large and somewhat longer than it is tall.

For two centuries the common, non-pedigree European stock that eventually gave rise to both American and British Shorthairs developed differently in the two countries, evolving into the two types that are reflected in today's pedigree breeds.

As might be expected from its origins, this breed has its full measure of intelligence and is both strong and athletic. It has a very strongly developed hunting instinct, which it exercises at every opportunity, even when fully fed.

Tabbies occur in all the recognized colors, and in both classic and mackerel patterns; there is no American equivalent, though, of its spotted British cousin.

A patched tabby is the agouti version of a tortoiseshell. Unlike the latter, which shows the underlying tabby pattern only in the paler colored areas (if they are large enough), the patched tabby shows it overall, running through the darker areas as well. In the UK it would be known as a tortie-tabby.

The first shorthair registered in the USA, in 1900, was a British import. A little British blood was introduced into selectively bred native street cats and by 1904 the first truly home-produced American Shorthair had been entered on the register.

Despite their self-sufficient nature, American Shorthairs make first class domestic pets. They are affectionate, home-loving and generally get on well with all members of the family, provided their individuality is respected.

As well as the Brown (genetically black), patched tabbies are also bred in the dilute Blue; a Silver version, in which the unmarked areas are simply tipped with color is also known.

This variety would be called Tortoiseshell and White in Britain. The white should predominate on the underparts and there must be no white flecking in the colored areas. Eye color is gold in all varieties of the breed except the White (blue, gold or odd) and Silvers (green/blue-green, or hazel in Silver Tabbies).

At first called simply the Shorthair, the breed was soon given the name of Domestic Shorthair (by which name it is still often known today). It received its current name in 1966, since when it has ranked among the top award winners.

Breeding the American Shorthair is uncomplicated. They are productive and easy to manage during pregnancy and when kittening. Litters typically consist of four kittens, which usually display the healthiness inherent in the breed.

The only other variety is the Dilute Calico in which the black and red colors are replaced by blue and cream. (Chocolate and lilac versions occur only in Exotic and British Shorthairs.)

This is one of the newest and rarest varieties. The pattern is named after the semi-longhaired Turkish breed that typifies it. The color, which can be any of the solid colors, calico or blue-cream, is largely restricted to the head and tail, though one or two small patches elsewhere are permissible.

In its early days the American Shorthair was eclipsed in terms of popularity by the Maine Coon Cat. Because of its humble origins it was at first more tolerated than admired at shows. Its standing improved greatly, however, in the 1940s and '50s.

It requires no special attention but the coat does benefit from an occasional brushing. As with all cats it is best to accustom kittens to this procedure early on. If started soon enough they do not take unkindly to a bath now and then as well.

The American Shorthair also has the usual bi-colored (solid color with white) varieties but it is one of the few shorthaired breeds in which the full van pattern is likely to be encountered.

The Bengal is a very rare, spotted breed of which only a few exist outside North America. It is a fairly large cat with a head that seems small in proportion to the long, highly muscular body. The hind legs are longer than the front and the paws are distinctively large. The thick coat comes in a range of colors.

Developed in the USA in the late 1970s from crosses between the Egyptian Mau and a wild species, the Asian Leopard Cat (*Felis bengalensis*), in an attempt to capture the aura of the latter in a domestic cat.

Despite its ancestor's reputation for ferocity it is affectionate and docile. Male offspring from matings between different species are sterile so Mau males are frequently used, but an individual's pedigree must show at least one-sixteenth wild ancestry.

The combination of head shape, medium ears, body type and large paws separate this cat from similarly marked breeds such as the Ocicat, Egyptian Mau and Spotted Tabby Oriental Shorthair.

CALIFORNIA SPANGLED Brown

USA & UK – breed not recognized

Like the Bengal, this is another very rare, exclusively spotted American cat. Its body is medium in size but long and slung low on strong legs. Paw size is average. The head is wide and full-muzzled. Colors of the short, velvety coat include black, brown, blue and red, and their silver and gold versions.

The California Spangled was created in America in the 1970s using a mixture of breeds, ostensibly as a memorial to all wild cats sacrificed to the fur trade. Though not officially recognized, it does have is own association of devotees.

The breed reputedly has above-average intelligence and is good tempered. Newborn kittens are black with white markings only on the chin, around the eyes and inside the ear; they develop the adult pattern and coloring as they grow.

The Bengal is perhaps the most similar breed but that has a less full muzzle, smaller ears, heavier paws and stands taller at the back. The Ocicat has larger ears and more rounded eyes.

The distinctive feature of this long-tailed, graceful cat is its short, dense, double coat that stands up from the skin. The guard hairs are lightly tipped with silver, giving it a velvet lustre. The green eyes may be round (US) or almond-shaped (UK). The UK standard also calls for prominent whisker pads.

Its true origin is obscure but is believed to have been brought to Britain from Russian ports by 17th and 18th century sailors. It was almost lost during the last war but concerted efforts in Britain and Scandinavia revived it. Formerly called the Maltese.

Russians make placid, often shy, but affectionate companions. The sparsely-furred, translucent ears (set higher on the head in UK as opposed to US examples) should be kept clean. White and Black varieties have preliminary recognition in the UK.

The coat texture is unlike that of any other breed. Green eyes further separate it from the gold/orange-eyed Chartreux and British and American Blue Shorthairs. (See also Korat.)

Like the Russian Blue, this is another green-eyed, blue breed but there the similarity ends. The face, with its oversized, round eyes, is heart-shaped. The single coat is glossy and close-lying, and the hairs so tipped with silver as to create a halo effect not seen in any other breed. There are no other varieties.

A rare, centuries-old, native breed from Thailand that was first imported from its homeland to the USA in 1959 and recognized there in 1966. Britain's first Korats came from America in 1972. To keep the breed pure no cross-breeding is permitted.

Korats are gentle pets that form a very strong bond with their owners. They have unusually highly developed senses and do not like sudden, loud noises but they are themselves rather talkative. The eye color is yellow up to two years old.

Shorter-tailed than the Russian Blue and with a quite different face. Its coat is similar only in color, not in texture or silvering. Green eyes further separate it from other blues of similar type.

OCICAT Chocolate
UK – breed not recognized

A large, man-made, exclusively spotted breed, virtually unknown in Britain, which has a very "jungle cat" look and is named from its resemblance to an Ocelot. The strongly ticked coat (each hair bears several agouti bands) may be in standard or silver versions of tawny, chocolate, cinnamon, blue, lavender or fawn.

It first appeared in 1964 as a surprise result from a US attempt to produce an Aby-pointed Siamese. Its pedigree includes Abyssinian, Siamese and American Shorthair. Accepted for registration in 1966 but not fully recognized until 1987.

The Ocicat shows dog-like devotion to its owner without being demanding. It is not shy and will welcome visitors. Intelligent and easily trained, it will retrieve, respond to commands and does not object to walking on the leash.

Most closely resembles the Egyptian Mau but perhaps more heavily ticked. Larger eared than most other spotted cats and different from Spotted Tabby Oriental Shorthairs in head conformation.

The only natural spotted breed. It has a long body, similar in type to the Abyssinian, with hind legs longer than front and a medium long tail. The head is a slightly rounded wedge shape with a medium length nose. The M mark on the forehead, fancifully called the scarab mark, is ornate in this breed.

Though their ancestry is believed to date back to the pharaohs, all today's Maus are descended from three cats (born in Italy in 1953 of parents taken from Egypt) that were imported to the US in 1956. The breed gained the CFA's full recognition in 1977.

The Mau (the Egyptian word for cat) is very intelligent and it makes an affectionate, devoted pet. Untemperamental, though some are said to shun strangers, it is well-behaved and has a soft, singing voice. It can be trained to the lead.

There are three varieties – bronze, silver and smoke. The similar Ocicat stands less high on the hind legs. The longer-nosed Spotted Tabby Oriental Shorthair is the only other large-eared, spotted cat.

A long-bodied cat, which ideally should have an average head type (some look too oriental), characterized by a short, glossy, colorpointed coat and white feet. The Seal variety tends to darker body coloring than the Siamese and may also show white on the muzzle and chest as well as a blaze on the nose.

This is a recent and still very rare American creation, also called Silver Laces, based on a Siamese/American Shorthair Bi-color cross to produce a colorpointed cat with white mittens. In effect it is a shorthaired, but more foreign, version of the Ragdoll.

The Snowshoe is said to have a very easygoing nature that combines the qualities of its parent breeds. It is even-tempered and affectionate but sometimes displays an extrovert, somewhat demanding side to its personality.

The combination of colored points and white feet is not found in any other shorthaired cat. The only other US variety is Seal Point. Similar cats in other colors are being bred in the UK.

The smallest of all breeds, the Singapura has distinctively large ears and a noticeable break between the cheeks and squarish muzzle. The all-over agouti coat is exceptionally short and close-lying, the hairs showing two bands of dark brown ticking on an ivory ground color. The underside is creamy-white.

Developed as a pedigree breed in the USA from three cats taken from the streets of Singapore (Singapura is the Malay name for that island) in 1975. It received full CFA recognition in 1988. Since 1989 small numbers have been exported to Britain.

Singapuras are very friendly cats. Playful even as adults, they are full of curiosity and have a habit of getting in the way of whatever their owner is doing. They make good mothers, often nursing their youngsters well beyond the age of independence.

The one color to date is known as sepia agouti. Another ticked tabby breed is the Abyssinian and the pattern is also found in the Oriental Shorthair and in the Asian group (see note 6, p.115).

ABYSSINIAN Ruddy

UK – Usual Abyssinian

The Abyssinian has a look unlike that of any other shorthair, due partly to its all-over ticked coat but also to its alert, wide-eyed expression, topped by the large, pricked ears. Of intermediate foreign type, it has a medium body, neither cobby nor tubular, and a fairly wedge-shaped head with a medium length nose.

Some regard the Aby as the cat depicted in ancient Egyptian art. Others think it is descended from a cat taken to Britain from Abyssinia in the late 1860s. There is little evidence for either theory but early belief in the latter has given the breed its name.

Though it may be shy at first, an Abyssinian quickly becomes people-oriented and displays a very strong loyalty to its owner; it will, however, often remain aloof with strangers. It enjoys company and will sulk if left too long on its own.

Only Ruddy (UK – Usual), Red (UK – Sorrel), Blue and Fawn are universally recognized. Chocolate, Lilac, and true, sex-linked Red and Cream varieties have preliminary recognition in Britain.

ABYSSINIAN Red

UK – Sorrel Abyssinian

The heavily ticked coat is a characteristic feature of the breed. It is, in fact, one of the four tabby patterns but the only marks are a solid tip to the tail, a reduced M on the forehead and a dark line round each eye. Poor examples may show barring on the legs, tail and chest. The eye color is amber to green.

Though the breed's true origins are unknown, recent genetic studies suggest that its homeland was the Indian Ocean coast. Wherever it came from, it was refined, perhaps even created, in Britain in the latter decades of the last century.

It is highly inquisitive, extremely intelligent. and, with persistent training, can be taught to play games – but always with dignity. Being an active and athletic cat it appreciates access to trees but is happy to accept furniture as a substitute.

The GCCF now gives preliminary recognition to tortoiseshell versions in all the colors (except sex-linked red and cream, of course) but none of these is recognized in America.

In the silver varieties the development of pigment is suppressed, particularly in the paler agouti bands on each hair. The coat retains the colored bands of ticking, largely unreduced at the hair tip but diluted lower down, thus giving an effect of colored flecks on a near-white ground carrying just a blush of color.

First exported to North America in the early 1900s, but not in any quantity or quality until the late 1930s, the breed's popularity is now exceeded only by Siamese and Burmese, and it is far more numerous there than in Britain.

The breed is not prolific and the litters commonly number only one to three. Like all shorthairs, the kittens are fluffy at first; they look almost solid-colored for a time, the ticking taking two or three months to show and then developing slowly after that.

UK recognition is provisional for Black, Sorrel and Blue Silvers, and preliminary for Chocolate, Lilac and Fawn Silvers. No silver varieties are recognized in America.

HAVANA BROWN

This breed and the Chestnut Oriental Shorthair (UK – Havana) had the same origin but while the British continued to cross it with Siamese, the Americans did not. Thus the two diverged. Its most distinctive feature is the square muzzle, with a definite stop and pronounced angle where it joins the cheeks.

Perpetuated from early imports of a 1950s British breed created by crossing a Seal Point Siamese with a black shorthair. It was recognized by the CFA in 1964. So named because its color (genetically chocolate) is reminiscent of that of Cuban cigars.

The Havana Brown is gentle and affectionate. It purrs loudly at the slightest encouragement but rarely uses its quiet voice, though it is vociferous when tending kittens. It is a compulsive "toucher," constantly playing with small household objects.

The only variety. Lacks the oriental type of the Chestnut Oriental Shorthair. Superficially similar to the Brown Burmese but that has quite different head conformation and yellow, not green, eyes.

This exclusively colorpointed breed shows the extreme of the foreign type: a medium-sized, long and graceful, almost tubular body; long, slim legs, the hind longer than the front; a long, thin tail; a tapering, wedge-shaped, long-nosed head bearing large ears and vivid blue, almond-shaped, slanting eyes.

Whether or not they originally hailed from elsewhere, Siamese cats are depicted in medieval documents from a former capital of Siam (now Thailand), where they were highly valued. By the 19th century only royalty was allowed to own them.

Brimming with personality, Siamese have a character all of their own. They are often unpredictable, being subject to mood swings that may alter daily. They become very devoted to their owners, jealously demanding attention all the time.

No other normal coated, shorthaired breed combines extreme foreign type with a colorpoint coat. The Snowshoe is perhaps the closest but that has white feet and a quite different head.

In all varieties the short, sleek, close-lying coat carries the named color (and pattern if there is one) only on the points i.e., the mask, ears, lower legs/feet and tail. It should be well defined against a much paler, but complementary, body color that may be shaded slightly on the back and sides.

By 1871 the breed had appeared in Britain and it reached America around 1890. Until the 1930s, when the Blue Point (historically probably a Seal Point/Korat hybrid) was accepted, Seal Point was the only recognized variety.

The Siamese is highly intelligent and very resourceful. It is quite capable of working out how best to get its own way. These qualities give it a dog-like ability to respond to training and it can be taught to do tricks, retrieve and walk on a lead.

Seal, Blue, Lilac (Frost) and Chocolate Points are universally recognized as Siamese. Other UK Siamese varieties are classed as a different breed, Colorpoint Shorthair, in the USA.

The founding members of the breed in the 19th century carried the requisite genes for the four classic colors. All the others, like the Red, have been created by crossing with other breeds. As the non-agouti gene is ineffectual on orange pigment faint tabby marks invariably show on Red and Cream Points.

The Red Point was developed in both the USA and the UK in the late 1940s. The CFA refused it recognition as a Siamese but in 1964 created a new breed, Colorpoint Shorthair, to accommodate it. It was recognized by the GCCF in 1966.

Though it is nervous and dislikes loud noises, the Siamese has the loudest voice of all cats. It is very agile and will climb trees and furniture with equal facility. Advice to would-be owners: if you have the time and can stand the pace, this is the ideal cat!

A dilute version of this variety, the Cream Point, also exists. The Red and Cream Points are outwardly identical to the tabby point versions in the same colors but are in fact genetically different.

COLORPOINT SHORTHAIR Chocolate-Lynx Point
UK – Chocolate-Tabby Point Siamese

The ideal Siamese head is an elongated triangular shape but it should not look pointed. Viewed from the front, and in profile, its edges are straight, with no stop and only a slight break between muzzle and cheeks. In face view the ears continue the line of the wedge shape. A slightly Roman nose is acceptable.

Tabby Points were bred experimentally in Sweden as early as 1924 but it was a further 35 years before they began to attract enough interest in Britain to support an application for official recognition; it was eventually granted in 1966.

Squint eyes and kinked tails were once regarded as natural characteristics of the breed but they are now considered to be faults. Nonetheless, many wanting a pet Siamese feel they add character and actively search for cats that show them.

Tabby points occur in all nine of the Siamese point colors (six in the USA). The GCCF recognizes Tortie-Tabby Points (in the same range of colors except red and cream) as well.

COLORPOINT SHORTHAIR Lilac-Cream Point
UK – Lilac Tortie Point Sianese

Under the influence of the Siamese gene pigmentation is temperature sensitive – the lower the temperature, the more pigment is produced. The skin at the extremities is slightly cooler than that over the body, hence the darker points. Cats reared in warmer environments commonly have paler coats.

New Siamese varieties recognized in the UK in 1994 include Cinnamon, Caramel and Fawn Points. Smoke (Shadow) Points, Tipped (Pastel Points) and Silver Tabby Points are being developed but as yet none is accepted in either the UK or USA.

Siamese and Colorpoint Shorthairs are precocious and prolific breeders. Females may be sexually mature at four or five months (but they should not be mated so young). Five or more kittens in a litter are not unusual. In all varieties they are born white.

Seal, Blue and Chocolate Tortie Point Colorpoint Shorthairs also occur (but as Siamese in the UK). Cinnamon, Caramel and Fawn Tortie Points have preliminary recognition in the UK only.

The original Siamese in the UK included some non-colorpoint cats with yellow/green eyes but from the late 1920s their breeding was discouraged. Interest in producing a range of such cats showing the extreme foreign type revived after the war and the Havana (genetically chocolate) was the first to be produced.

It originated in the UK in 1952 from a Siamese/black shorthair cross and was recognized in 1958. Blood from the Foreign White program improved the desired type and the standard was amended in 1974. (See also Havana Brown p.87.)

This and the other extreme foreign-type shorthairs that follow (called Oriental Shorthairs in the US) now differ from Siamese only in respect of one or two color genes. In general form, temperament and personality they are therefore virtually identical to that breed.

Nine further solid colors are bred. This and the remaining cats in the shorthair section have a body type that separates them from nearly all other similarly colored/patterned cats.

With its lean lines, pure white, close-lying coat, large pricked ears and pink nose, the White Oriental Shorthair is a strikingly elegant example of breeders' skills. In the UK standard the eyes are described as a clear, brilliant blue but the American standard also permits green or odd eyes.

The breeding of non-colorpoint Siamese-type cats gathered momentum in 1962 when a concerted effort was made to create this blue-eyed, all-white variety. By 1965 it was being admired at shows but full recognition was not granted until 1977.

Reputedly this variety does not suffer from the deafness to which many white cats are prone (the gene that causes the defect normally accompanies the white color but selective breeding from only hearing individuals can minimize its effect).

In the USA an all-white cat that is genetically fully Siamese is known and may be registered as Albino Siamese; it is almost identical to the White Oriental Shorthair but has paler blue eyes.

The color of this female-only variety is a frosty, pinkish-gray intermingled with shades of cream. Like most of the Oriental Shorthairs, the varieties in the Tortoiseshell group have green eyes. In red, cream and tortie varieties within the Shaded, Tipped and Tabby groups it may be copper to green but the latter is preferred.

The White program produced cats in other colors that have been used to create a large range, including tortoiseshells. Americans began breeding their own Oriental Shorthairs in 1968 and the breed was recognized here in 1977.

The well known Siamese squint is a fault that can also show up in some Oriental Shorthairs. It is thought to be the cat's attempt to correct double vision caused by irregularities in the nerve connections between the eyes and the brain.

Tortoiseshell Oriental Shorthairs are bred in seven of the nine colors (red or cream tortoiseshells are genetically impossible). Calico and Blue-Cream Calico are also recognized in America.

ORIENTAL SHORTHAIR Blue Silver
UK – Blue Silver Shaded Oriental

A short to medium-length colored tip on the guard hairs creates the Shaded group, which contains standard (paler base color) and silver (white base color) varieties. The color lies as a mantle on the body – darker on the back, shading to paler towards the underside. The tip color is reduced in Silvers.

In 1970 an accidental Chinchilla/Siamese cross produced a shaded silver kitten of foreign type that was the founder of a whole range of Oriental Shorthair Smokes, and Shadeds, and also contributed to Oriental Shorthair silver tabbies and tipped Siamese.

Orientals develop early but it is advisable to wait until they are about a year old before allowing them to breed. Litters are relatively large, often numbering five to nine. The kittens develop quickly and are very active.

Members of this group can be in any of the nine Siamese point colors, seven tortoiseshell combinations or the silver versions of either. All have preliminary UK recognition (fewer in USA).

The various tabby patterns are very precisely defined in the standards. That for the Spotted requires the marks to be round, separate and evenly distributed. There should be a scarab mark on the forehead. The tail is ringed, with a solid tip. Barring is allowed on the legs but a solid spine line is a serious fault.

Created in the UK in the 1960s using tabby point Siamese and Havanas. Originally called Egyptian Mau, its name was changed on recognition in 1978 to avoid confusion with the American breed of that name, which has a different origin (see p.81).

Like Siamese, Oriental Shorthairs – Spotted Tabbies included – are not for the faint-hearted. They are all demanding, vocal cats that love attention. The owner's rewards are great, however, because they are most affectionate, loyal and entertaining.

Also bred as classic, mackerel and ticked tabbies (plus their tortie versions) in all colors, giving a possible 128 varieties, most of which have as yet less than full recognition in the UK.

MANX Calico
UK – Tortie & White Manx

The body of a Manx cat is solid and short, with a well-rounded rump carried higher than the shoulders because of the much longer hind legs. This gives it a curious, rabbit-like, bobbing gait. The head is large, round and only slightly longer than it is broad. The lack of a tail is, of course, its most distinctive feature.

The Isle of Man in the UK is accepted as the home of this breed but when or where it really did originate is not known. Tailless cats of various types and from many places have been recorded but only this one, from Isle of Man stock, has been developed.

Intelligent, playful and affectionate, the members of this breed make first class family pets. The lack of a tail with which to communicate seems to have encouraged more expressive body language than most cats display. They are ruthless mousers.

Complete taillessness is unique to the Manx among recognized breeds. The gene mutation that causes it, however, can occur spontaneously in other breeds but this is extremely rare.

Fully tailless examples have a definite hollow at the end of the spine but varying degrees of taillessness are possible (see next page). The Manx has a double coat that should show a marked difference in texture between the durable, glossy top coat and the softer undercoat, giving it a well-padded feel.

Despite the many picturesque legends about how this cat lost its tail the deficiency is in fact the result of a mutant gene. A Manx club was formed in 1901 and the breed has been recognized since the cat fancy's early days in both America and Britain.

The effect of the Manx gene is not always restricted to the tail with the result that within the breed there is a relatively high incidence of skeletal abnormality such as spina bifida. It is also responsible for more still births and kitten deaths than are usual.

The British standard allows Manx to be any combination of color and pattern except colorpoint. In North America lilac and chocolate are also excluded.

A Stumpie Manx has a definite but short tail that may be curved or kinked. A shorter version (rumpy-riser) in which the tail is a mere inconspicuous knob also exists. In the UK both these can be registered but are not entered in cat shows. In the USA the latter may be shown alongside fully tailless (rumpy) cats.

The genetics of taillessness dictate that Manx offspring will display it in varying degrees. Four types are possible, from none (rumpies) to almost normal (longies), as well as some that have wholly normal tails. Stumpies are an intermediate group.

Despite the congenital problems to which the breed is prone (and which would almost certainly disqualify it from recognition were it a modern development), it is obviously vigorous enough to have survived unaided for several hundred years.

Similar to the relatively unknown American Bobtail but has smaller ears and different stance. The only other short-tailed breed, the Japanese Bobtail, is decidedly different in type.

In effect this is a true-breeding, semi-longhaired version of the Manx to which it is otherwise genetically identical. The soft coat is double but falls smoothly even so. The hair length gradually increases from shoulders to rump. Breeches and a ruff are evident, and ear and toe tufts desirable.

In the late 1960s longhaired kittens appeared spontaneously in some normal Manx litters in Canada. Careful selective breeding fixed the long coat as a true-breeding feature and its wearers were given the new name. Provisionally recognized by the CFA.

The Cymric (named for obscure reasons from the celtic word for Wales) has a similar temperament to a Manx. It is another of those breeds that are said to be dog-like in that its loyalty tends to center on one person and it responds well to training.

As it carries the Manx gene it can occur with any length of tail but only tailless forms are shown. Most colors/patterns are acceptable except chocolate, lilac and colorpoint.

The American Bobtail has a stocky body, carried low to the ground, and a broad, rounded head with medium to large ears. The tail is only 1–4 inches (2.5–10cm) long and may end in a small, tight curve. The plush, silky coat is essentially that of a semi-longhair but in can vary in length to medium-short.

A new, experimental breed that has a relatively small following in the USA. It arose in the 1960s from a cross between a Seal Point Siamese and a short-tailed tabby of unknown parentage. Birman and Himalayan blood was later incorporated.

It is said to have a delightful personality and to enjoy human company. No breeding problems are reported but fully tailless and long-tailed versions seem to be possible; whether the Manx gene may be involved has not been established.

All colors and patterns are allowed; it is the only short-tailed breed with colorpointed members. Completely tailless and longer-tailed examples are not considered acceptable.

This is a sturdy, medium-sized cat with a body type that could be described as foreign but is not classically so. The unique tail, 4–5 inches (10–12cm) long is corkscrew-curled; this disturbs the lie of the fur and gives it a pom-pom look. Mi-ke (meaning "three fur") is a calico; usually the white element is predominant.

Bobtailed cats have existed in Japan for many centuries. They were considered lucky and many families owned one. Japanese fanciers largely ignored them, however, until 1963 when visiting American judges much admired the local pet cats.

The Japanese Bobtail has an unusually varied but gentle voice and is very talkative. It makes an ideal, friendly pet. The kittens, usually four, are large when born and develop more quickly than in most breeds; even so, the mother tends them for longer.

Any color or pattern is allowed (except colorpoint or ticked tabby) but the Mi-ke, and the solid colors, bi-colors and tortoiseshell that can be used to create it, are preferred.

103

The head in this breed is distinctive: triangular, fairly long and large-eared but, for all that, lacking the classic oriental look. The eyes are slightly slanted, cheek bones notably high and the profile gently dished. Patterned cats (in solid-, bi- or tri-colors) show tabby marks, with or without areas of solid color.

In 1968 a number were taken from Japan to the USA, where they soon became popular, and they successfully survived the recognition procedure between 1971 and 1976. The breed is still virtually unknown in Europe, however.

Unlike the Manx, the Japanese Bobtail breeds true, producing consistently short-tailed offspring. Kitten mortality is low and the breed has a high resistance to disease. Clearly, the short-tail gene responsible is not the same as that operating in the Manx.

The combination of the short tail and distinctive but individual foreign type is unique. Both Stumpy Manx and American Bobtails are totally different in head and body conformation.

A medium-sized cobby cat with both British and American Shorthairs in its pedigree. It has a plush, upstanding coat, a round head and a wide-eyed expression topped by distinctive forward- and downward-folded ears. It is rare in Britain but popular, though not numerous, in America.

The folded ear first appeared as a spontaneous mutation in a Scottish farm kitten in 1961. Its descendants were registered and shown in the UK but were subsequently banned on health grounds in the early 1970s. Recognized by the CFA in 1978.

Folds make gentle and affectionate pets. They are hardy but if mated together can produce offspring hampered by a thickening of the limbs and tail. Ear mite infestation can be avoided by the normal hygiene that any owner should practice.

Any color and pattern is acceptable except chocolate, lilac or colorpoint. The Scottish Fold is the only breed of cat with ears that fold forward.

In this, one of the newest of recognized breeds, ears that curve gently backwards are the unique feature. The degree of curl may vary between individuals and its genetic basis dictates that some offspring will have normal ears. Both shorthaired and semi-longhaired coats are allowed within the standard.

In 1981 two kittens born to a black, semi-longhaired stray in southern California were seen to have backward-curling ears. Selective breeding perpetuated this spontaneous mutation. The CFA gave the new breed provisional recognition in 1991.

All kittens are born with straight ears but the curling begins in two to ten days. At six weeks the ears are tightly curled but then begin to unfurl, reaching their set position at four to six months. Curls are said to make adaptable, home-loving and playful pets.

All colors and patterns, including colorpoint, are permitted. Shorthaired, normal-eared individuals most closely resemble American Shorthairs but have a slightly more foreign body type.

This medium to large breed closely conforms in most respects to its cousin the American Shorthair and from a distance might well be taken for one. Up close, however, there is no mistaking the coat, the hairs of which are crimped, hooked or bent and in the longer areas form small ringlets rather than waves.

The wirehair coat first appeared as a spontaneous mutation in a single kitten born to a pair of New York State farm cats in 1966. A program was started and a true-breeding line established. Accepted for registration in 1966 and fully recognized in 1978.

The rather scruffy look of the breed in no way detracts from its charm, indeed many feel it adds to it. It is quiet but affectionate, inquisitive and playful, and a good mouser. An independent streak protects it from over-zealous dogs and children.

The texture of the crimped coat is unique among cats. It differs from that of the Cornish and Devon Rexes, which feel soft, in being springy and quite hard to the touch.

The Cornish Rex is the result of a spontaneous mutation that affects the development of the coat hairs. Guard hairs are absent and awn hairs modified to be like the naturally wavy down hairs. These give the coat a ripple effect known (from 1920s hairdressing terminology) as a marcel wave.

The foundation cat for this breed was born on a Cornwall farm in 1950. The name used for a similar mutation in rabbits was adopted. A genetically identical mutation had occurred in Germany in 1946 but was not taken up by breeders until 1951.

Though it may look like a cat for the specialist, the Cornish is an excellent family pet. It has an extrovert personality and a high level of intelligence. Devoted and affectionate, it gets on well with dogs and children but less so with cats of other breeds.

Cornish and Devon Rexes both have short, waved coats but that of the Devon is very slightly coarser. In head conformation the two are quite different, the Devon's being more pixie-like.

Because of the lack of guard hairs the overall hair length is about half that of normal shorthairs and similarly less dense. This gives it a remarkably soft, silky feel. Stroking these cats brings another surprise because they feel much warmer than other breeds. The whiskers are shortened and curly as well.

The breed was recognized by the GCCF in 1967. Two cats from the UK were sent to the USA in 1957 and a German Rex in 1960. Initially Cornish were not distinguished from Devon Rexes in the USA but separate recognition did come in 1979.

The lithe, muscular body and long hind legs make the Rex particularly agile and acrobatic. It is able to move very suddenly and amazingly fast, even when it looks to be totally relaxed. Such capabilities make it a very skilled hunter.

The only other recognized crinkly/wavy-coated breed is the American Wirehair with a quite different conformation and coat texture. The rex gene and wirehair gene are not the same.

In type this breed is decidedly foreign but of a version all its own. The slender, medium-length, hard and muscular body is borne on long, slim, straight legs, which, with its arched stance, makes it look tall. The tail is long, thin and whippy. The head is small, foreign in type but with full cheeks and a muzzle break.

Similar rex mutations have occurred spontaneously elsewhere but none has become established as a separate breed. Two such strains (resembling the Cornish) appeared in Ohio (1953) and Oregon (1964) but both are now believed to be extinct.

The coat of this breed needs little attention and does not shed. Its sparseness, however, does mean that the cat is sensitive to cold. To counteract this some owners supplement the diet with high-energy fat. Three to six is the usual litter size.

Cornish Rexes are bred in any and all colors, with or without white markings. Those showing the Siamese pattern are sometimes referred to as Si-Rexes, not colorpoints.

Like that of the Cornish Rex, the coat is formed into rippled waves, caused by modification of the hairs. Here the guard hairs are present but changed, as are awn hairs more to resemble down hairs. On the underparts the fur may be reduced to a mere fuzz of down. Whiskers are often much shortened or even absent.

The progenitor of today's members of this breed was a feral cat found living in a decommissioned Devon (England) tin mine in 1960. The line he established was recognized by the GCCF as a separate breed from the Cornish Rex in 1967 and by the CFA in 1979.

Both Rex breeds have a similar personality and behavior. They are highly curious, refuse to be left out of anything and will trot, not walk, after their owner everywhere. Both are very dog-like, even to the extent of wagging their tails when pleased.

The full range of coat colors and patterns is acceptable. As in the Cornish Rex, eye color should be complementary to coat color but in Si-Rex varieties only Siamese blue is allowed.

The wedge-shaped head is full-cheeked with a short but well delineated muzzle bearing prominent whisker pads. Wide-open, large eyes and huge, low-set ears accentuate this cat's unique, impish look. The medium length, slender body is carried high on long, slim legs and though it looks fragile is hard and muscular.

Although the spontaneous mutation responsible for this breed has a similar effect on the coat to the Cornish one, the two genes are in fact different. This is proved by the fact that a Cornish/Devon cross produces only normal-coated offspring.

These cats rarely shed and then only lightly. The beautifully soft coat is easy to maintain but if necessary most Rexes do not object to a bath. They chat merrily in chirps and trills and purr loudly. Kittens (usually four) are precocious and highly mobile!

As well as having different head conformation to the Cornish Rex, neither is the coat quite the same, the Devon's being a little more sparse and slightly less curled.

112

In this cat the coat is limited to a suede-like covering only on the points and testicles. Elsewhere it is virtually naked but the skin carries pigmentation in near-normal colors and patterns (any are acceptable). The head is similar to a Devon Rex's but a different gene (again a spontaneous mutation) is involved here.

The breed was developed from an almost hairless kitten born to a Canadian house cat in 1966. Early recognition in Canada was short-lived and it is now recognized only by one of the smaller US bodies. In Europe it is known only in Holland and France.

Said to be an affectionate cat that enjoys company. It is also at home with dogs and like them (and Rexes) wags its tail when happy. Obviously at a disadvantage in cold conditions, it should then be protected, even to the extent of wearing a knitted coat.

Bald cats have been recorded several times in the past but only one other achieved named status, the Mexican Hairless Cat, which died out early this century. The Sphynx is now unique.

Paw-notes

 Persian (pp.14 & 20) Turkish cats (pp.48–9) Angora (UK) (pp.53–4)

The original Angora was a very ancient breed, taken to Europe from Turkey in the 1500s. By the end of the 19th century another imported longhaired cat, the Persian (now called simply the Long Hair in the UK), had surpassed it in popularity. Breeders tried to improve the Persian coat by crossing with the silky-coated Angora, whose type was by then considered inferior, and as a result the identity of the latter was lost. By the early 1900s it had died out as a separate breed. In the 1950s and '60s revival of western interest in native longhairs from Turkey resulted in the recognition of the Turkish Angora in the USA and the Turkish Van in the UK. These may well evoke memories of the original Angoras but the relationship is merely that they are longhaired, bear some resemblance in type and originate from Turkey; beyond that there can now be no proof that they are genetically the same breed. The modern Angora in Britain (called Oriental Longhair in the US) was also likened to the original Angora, hence its name, but no relationship between the two breeds is claimed. US Turkish Angoras and UK Angoras differ in both origin and type and are unrelated breeds. The Turkish Van (given preliminary recognition by the CFA in 1988) and Turkish Angora do differ somewhat in type but may simply be strains of the same breed that over the years have developed along slightly different lines because of geographical isolation in their homeland.

 Peke-face Persian (p.34)

Some UK breeders are now producing Long Hairs with heads that not only reach the extremes of the Persian type as laid down in the breed standard but sometimes go beyond them. The face is flat and the nose is extremely short and pushed upwards. These are known as Ultra-type Long Hairs, or simply Ultras, and they are becoming dangerously close to being indistinguishable from the unrecognized Peke-face variety.

 Tiffanie (p.40)

In the 1970s longhaired cats with the Burmese brown (sable) color were developed in North America and the breed were given the name Tiffany (though it is not yet recognized by the CFA). When longhaired cats of Burmese type appeared among the descendants of the Burmese/Chinchilla accidental cross of 1981 in Britain they were thought to equate to the Tiffany and were given the same name (but a different spelling because Tiffany had previously been registered with the GCCF as a breeder's prefix and was therefore unavailable for use as a breed name). There is now some doubt that the two do represent the same breed. Documentation of the true origins of the US Tiffany seems to have been lost. Certainly its bloodlines are not the same as those of its UK "counterpart" and there is even a suggestion that it had ancestors in common with the UK Angora but was subsequently developed along less oriental lines. Burmese brown is the most common Tiffany (US) color but the gene that gives rise to it is independent of the Burmese type and there is now doubt as to whether the American breed of this name has any Burmese (breed) ancestry at all.

 Balinese/Javanese (p.52) Angora/Oriental Longhair (pp.53/4)

In the USA the longhaired version of the Siamese is allowed to be registered as Balinese only in the classic Siamese colors of seal, blue chocolate and lilac; all other colors (including tortoiseshells) and any showing a tabby pattern must be registered as a separate breed, Javanese. Do not be confused by the fact that the European organization FIFe, and societies affiliated to it (including some British ones), use the name Javanese for the breed that the GCCF knows as the Angora and that in the USA is called the Oriental Longhair.

5 **British/European Short Hair (p.61)**

British cat fanciers compiled standards for pedigree cats before the continental Europeans began to do the same. The name British Short Hair therefore has some precedence but, not unnaturally, European Shorthair is used on the continent even though the cats are essentially the same. Indeed, many European Shorthairs are cats taken there from Britain, and certainly British cats have been used to improve European strains. There may be varieties of European Shorthair, however, that are not recognized as British Short Hairs, for example the Albino.

Tiffanie (p.40) Bombay (p.68) Burmilla (p.69)

In the UK the Bombay, Burmilla and Tiffanie are regarded as members of the Asian Group, which contains all cats that are of Burmese type but non-Burmese coat length, color or pattern. All members of the group, except the Tiffanie, are given the same breed number by the GCCF. The individually named Bombay is the black member of the Asian solid-color sub-group within which blue, chocolate, lilac, red, cream, caramel or apricot examples can exist (but most of these and their tortie versions are experimental). The Burmillas are another sub-group; they formerly occurred in shell (tipped) or shaded forms in any of the above colors but the distinction between the two lengths of tipping was dropped in 1994. A smoke version of the Burmilla had the pre-recognition name of Burmoiré but is now another Asian sub-group known simply as Asian Smoke. The sub-group comprising the Tiffanie can be in any color or pattern found in the Asian group. Four further Asian sub-groups exist – one for each of the tabby patterns, classic, mackerel, spotted and ticked; members of each of these can be in any of the Asian colors or in the tortie-tabby form, or in the silver version of either. Asian tabbies are rising in popularity and were given provisional recognition in 1994. Any color within the Asian Group can be modified to its Burmese color equivalent under the effect of the Burmese gene. This can affect any member but will be most noticeable in genetically black cats, whose color will be modified to Burmese brown. When it occurs in the self group its effect is to produce cats that are identical in appearance to Burmese; these can be registered as Asian Variants but cannot be shown.

Egyptian Mau (p.81)

Do not confuse this breed with one created in Britain that was once called Egyptian Mau because of its believed resemblance to the ancient breed. The latter can still be found under that name in some books but is now more properly named Oriental Spotted Tabby (UK name) in recognition of its more extreme foreign type (see p.97).

Siamese (pp.88–92)

The genetics of the Oriental Shorthairs (see pp.93–7 and note 9 below) are such that cats identical in appearance to Siamese (any variety) may appear in certain strains. In the USA these can be registered as Oriental Shorthairs but in the UK they can be registered and shown as Siamese, to which they are, in fact, genetically identical. For identification purposes the difference is academic but it is important to breeders. (See also p.94.)

Oriental Shorthairs (pp.93–7)

Each of the cats on these pages are single representatives of what are regarded in Britain as separate breed groups whose mutual affinity is recognized by gathering them together within a sub-section termed Oriental Short Hair that contains nearly 200 possible varieties; in the USA they are all considered to be varieties of a single breed, the Oriental Shorthair, in which over 100 varieties are recognized. Until recently the UK breed name for nearly all self-colored, shorthaired cats of Siamese type was simply Foreign (e.g. Foreign Blue), the name Oriental being reserved for non-selfs. Currently, however, all non-colorpoint cats of this type have Oriental as at least part of their breed name except the Havana (for a time called the Chestnut Brown Foreign), which has been allowed to retain its traditional name, and the Foreign White, because it is the only blue-eyed variety in the range.

Oriental Shorthair Tabbies (p.97)

The different tabby patterns are classed as separate breeds in the UK (e.g. Oriental Classic Tabby, Oriental Spotted Tabby) but as varieties within the one breed (Oriental Shorthair) in the USA, where fewer are recognized than in Britain but still number over 50 possible color/pattern combinations, including patched tabbies and various silver versions.

Cornish/German Rex (p.108)

Although the same rex gene operates in Cornish and German Rex strains, European examples of the latter have been regarded as a separate breed since 1982 because their type is more like that of the European Shorthair. The German Rex's identity in America was lost in the early days because it was interbred with Cornish Rexes whose type prevailed.

Colors and patterns

The basic cat is the **tabby**, with its pattern of broad, black stripes separated by black-flecked, yellow-brown areas. In those areas between the stripes the black pigment on each guard hair is separated by one or more straw-colored bands – the so-called agouti bands. Because of these, in genetic terms, a tabby is known as an **agouti** cat. Modifications of the tabby pattern, the black pigment and the form in which it is expressed, and the presence and/or extent of the agouti bands gives us well over 2,000 theoretically possible varieties, each one the product of a combination of relatively few genes. Fortunately no breed possesses nearly as many varieties as this; a very few have just a single one but some do have as many as 200 or even more.

Colors

The black gene can exist in two other forms, which give the colors chocolate and cinnamon. One or other of these three is always present but will be completely masked if the gene for red is operating. A separate gene can act to dilute any of these four colors to blue, lilac, fawn and cream respectively. Yet another gene can act to modify the effect of the dilution gene to give varying shades of caramel (derived from black, chocolate or cinnamon) and apricot (derived from red).

CAT COLORS   Usual colors are shown above the diagonal and the Burmese variation, if applicable, below it. Siamese variation shades are similar to Burmese. The actual shade of any color can vary from cat to cat.

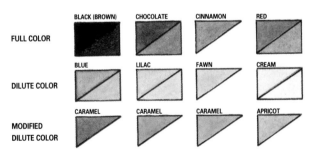

The expression of any of these ten colors can be influenced by the presence of either the Burmese gene or the Siamese gene. Both of these are named after the breeds that typify the colors they produce but either gene can theoretically operate in any breed. Both impart a lighter tone to the whole range and also cause the pigment to be temperature sensitive so that it is darker on the cooler extremities (points) of the cat. In coats influenced by the Burmese gene the contrast between the points and the rest of the body is slight (darker ears and mask may be the only sign) but it is much more pronounced in those so-called **colorpoint** cats where the Siamese gene is operating (see p.92). Note that the Burmese version of black is called sable (brown in the UK) and the Siamese version is seal. The variation of the usual colors and their dilute versions that is shown by the Abyssinian and Somali breeds results from the influence of special genes, which impart a red hue to the whole range. The color of the genetic black Abyssinian is known as ruddy (or "usual" in the UK) and that of the genetic cinnamon is called sorrel in the UK but, confusingly, red in the USA.

Approximate representations of these colors are shown in the chart opposite. Whichever one is present in an individual it will be totally masked if the dominant white gene is operating, when an all-white cat will be the result. If a color is not specified in a variety's name it is usually safe to assume that it will be black. Note also that in North America lilac is commonly called lavender (or frost in colorpointed cats), Burmese chocolate is champagne and Burmese lilac is platinum.

Tabbies and Selfs
In all cats one of three forms of a tabby pattern gene is always present. The most common is the **classic** or **blotched** tabby with broad markings. The **mackerel** tabby has narrower stripes. The third form is the **ticked** tabby (also called Abyssinian tabby but this form is not restricted to the breed that typifies it), which has all-over agouti hairs, the only marking being a suggestion of the "M" mark on the forehead that is common to all tabbies. A fourth form of tabby, the **spotted**, is thought to be a version of the mackerel form in which the stripes have become broken up. By convention the color of a genetically black tabby is known as brown (from the color of the agouti areas, not the stripes).

Though all cats are genetically one of the tabby forms, a gene may be present that removes the agouti bands on the hairs in the paler areas, leaving on the full length of each hair only the darker pigment, which is, of course, the same color as the markings. The result is a so-called **self** cat that has a uniformly solid-colored coat throughout. The non-agouti gene, however, is ineffective on red, cream or apricot. Uniformly colored cats in these colors are therefore very difficult to produce; the inherent tabby pattern can only be weakened by selective breeding.

Tortoiseshells and tortie-tabbies
The gene for red is carried on the X-chromosome, of which females have two (one from each parent) but males only one (which can be from either parent). Because of this imbalance one of the female's X-chromosomes is switched off at an early stage in embryonic development; in each cell of the embryo it is a matter of chance whether the chromosome derived from the male parent becomes ineffective or whether it is that from the female parent. Genes carried on this chromosome are therefore inherited differently by the two sexes and because of this they are said to be sex-linked.

When the red gene is inherited from both parents, offspring of either sex will be red tabby (whether agouti or non-agouti as explained above); but when it derives from only one parent male offspring will be red tabby but female embryos will become a mosaic of cells, some containing the red gene, others not. The coat of such females therefore becomes a patchwork of two colors, one of them red (or cream or apricot) and the other black, chocolate or cinnamon (or their dilute or modified dilute versions). Cats in these color combinations are **tortoiseshells** and, except in certain abnormal cases, are always female. In certain breeds the name of the blue version does not include the word tortoiseshell but is simply given as blue-cream, the name of its two constituent dilute colors.

The distribution of the two colors in any tortoiseshell is variable. In some cases the areas are small and intermingled (favored in Britain), in others they form larger patches (favored in the USA). In non-agouti cats the darker areas will be solid-colored but the paler red (or red-derived) areas will show their tabby pattern if they are large enough. That tabby pattern can be any of the four forms mentioned above. In agouti cats the effect will be an all-over tabby pattern (of any form) in the two colors; these are known in the UK as **tortie-tabbies** and in the USA as **patched tabbies** (sometimes as **torbies**).

White spotting

This is the name of the gene responsible for the presence of white, to any degree short of total, in any of the coats mentioned previously. Modifying genes control the extent to which it is expressed. The degree can range from a single white locket through white feet to the so-called **van pattern**, classically demonstrated by the Turkish Van breed, in which the coat is all white except for the tail and areas on the head. Less extensive white areas on an otherwise solid color produce the variety group known as **bi-color**. In North America the **tortoiseshell-and-white** variety is given the name **calico**.

Tipped coats

Two further genes can be present that, together or individually, produce a whole family of variations that can affect any of the coats mentioned so far (except in the all-white cat). These are the wide-band and inhibitor genes, which, though they operate in different ways, both have the effect of restricting the pigment, to a greater or lesser degree, to the tip of the hair. The term tipped is used in this book to refer to all such coats but it should be understood that this word is often used in a more restricted sense, particularly within the British cat fancy.

The wide-band gene is effective only in genetically agouti cats. It widens the agouti band in the paler areas of the tabby coat and converts the hairs in the solid, marked areas to agouti hairs that have similarly widened bands. Thus the tabby pattern is much dissipated or, in the best examples, lost almost completely. When the expression of this gene is strong the length of the pigmented hair tip is short, giving **standard shell** (or, in Britain, **standard tipped**) varieties; when it is weak the tip is longer and **standard shaded** varieties result. The distinction between the two is made in some breeds but in most the length of tip is not considered important and all examples are known simply as **shaded**. The color of the hair behind the tip is a paler version of the nominal color and affected coats have a more delicate, pastel appearance than their normal counterparts. In some breeds the genetically black varieties in this group are given the name **golden**. Tortie-tabbies can be affected but as the tabby pattern is lost they are known simply as **shell (tipped)** or **shaded torties**.

The inhibitor gene, when present, is effective in both agouti and non-agouti cats. In areas of solid color it bleaches the basal part of each hair, which then appears white with a long colored tip. The agouti hairs between the markings in a tabby pattern are bleached to white except at the extreme tip. In a non-agouti cat the result is a **smoke** or **tortie smoke** and in an agouti cat it is a **silver tabby** or **silver tortie-tabby**. In smokes the contrast between the surface color and the white base color is most pronounced when the coat parts as the cat moves.

When these two genes occur in combination the result (seen only in agouti cats) is **shell silver** (or simply **tipped** in the UK) and **shaded silver** (and their tortoiseshell versions). Shell coats are white with just a blush of color, whereas shaded coats are darker, shading to white on the underside. The black shell variety in some breeds is known as **chinchilla**, and the red or cream shell or shaded (and sometimes the tortoiseshells) as **cameos**. In the Long Hair and Exotic breeds orange-eyed versions of the green-eyed shaded silvers are called **pewters**.

Eye colors

The color of the iris is another variable characteristic. It can range from deep orange through amber and green to deep blue. The standard of all breeds specifies which eye color is acceptable and it may differ between varieties within the same breed. This feature is mentioned in the book only where it is particularly relevant.

Though they are not infallible the following generalisations may be made: all-white varieties of any breed and Turkish Van – blue, orange or odd (one blue, one orange); colorpoint varieties of any breed, including Siamese – deep blue; Korat, Russian Blue and silver varieties of any breed – green; Burmese and Asian group (including Bombay, Burmilla and Tiffanie) – yellow to yellow-green; Oriental Shorthair – green; Abyssinian and Somali – amber, hazel or green; Tonkinese – blue-green to light blue; most others – deep orange to amber.

Examples of some of the coat patterns commonly encountered are shown on the endpapers of the book. The chart overleaf summarises the range of varieties that are currently accepted for each breed; further notes on the chart and how to use it can be found on page 122.

RANGE OF COLORS AND PATTERNS THROUGHOUT THE BREEDS

Breed names in capitals are those recognized in the GCCF in the UK and, except for the Tiffanie, by the CFA in America – though not always in the full color range indicated. Breeds in normal type are recognized by the CFA but not by the GCCF. Those in smaller normal type are not recognized by either body but are recognized by smaller organizations.

Notes explaining this chart and how to use it are on page 122.

page	Breed	classic	mackerel	spotted	ticked	solid	tabby	van	colorpoint solid	colorpoint tabby	standard shell	standard shaded	silver shell	silver shaded	silver smoke	silver tabby
102	American Bobtail					all colors and patterns acceptable										
98-100	MANX		•			all colors and patterns acceptable except colorpoint										
108-110	CORNISH REX					all colors and patterns acceptable										
111-112	DEVON REX					all colors and patterns acceptable										
113	Sphynx					the skin carries some pigmentation which may be in any color or pattern										
76	Bengal			•		genetics not yet elucidated; brown (several variations) and blue varieties are known										
77	California Spangled			•		genetics not yet elucidated; black and brown (and variations of both), blue and red varieties are known										
81	Egyptian Mau			•			AC							A		
80	Ocicat			•			K							K		
46-47	SOMALI				•		L^T							L^T		
84-86	ABYSSINIAN				•		L^T									
83	Singapura				•		A									
14-34	PERSIAN (LONG HAIR)[1]	•				WJ^{T,W}	J^{T,W}	J^T	J^T	J^T		A	AF	E^{a}F	J^T	A
55-57	EXOTIC SHORTHAIR	•	•	•		WJ^{T,W}	J^{T,W}	J^T	J^T	J^T		A	J^T	E^{a}	J^T	A
58-63	BRITISH SHORTHAIR	•	•	•		WJ^{T,W}	J^T	J^T	J^T	J^T		A	J^T	J^T	J^T	J^T
106	American Curl[2]	•	•	•	•	WJ^{T,W}	G^T		J^T	J^T	A	A	A^TD	A^TD	J	J^T
58-64	ORIENTAL LONGHAIR	•	•	•												

120

Page	Breed	Coat/other columns (•)	Colour & variety codes (read left→right across colour columns)
68-69	ASIAN³ (UK name)	• • •	A · AD · AD · AD · A · ED · ED · ED · ED · E · ED · A · NT · NT
93-97	ORIENTAL SHORTHAIR⁴	• •	WMT · GT,W · GT,W · GT,W · GT,W · GT · MT · MT
44-45	NORWEGIAN FOREST CAT	• •	WGT,W · GT,W · GT,W · GT,W · GT,W · GT,W · GT,W
41-43	MAINE COON CAT	• •	WGT,W · GT,W · GT,W · GT,W · GT,W · GT,W
71-75	American Shorthair	• •	WGT,W · GT · GT · AD · AD · GT,W
107	American Wirehair	• •	WGT,W · GW · GW · AD · AD
101	Cymric	• •	WGT,W · GT · A · A · AT
105	Scottish Fold	• •	WGT,W · GT · ED · ED · ED · ATD · ATD · AT · ATD
48	Turkish Angora	• •	WGT,W · G · A · E · ED · A
103-104	Japanese Bobtail	• •	WGT,W · GT,W · AD · AD · A · AT · AT · AW · AW
88-92	SIAMESE⁵	• • •	MT · MT · MT · MT · MT
50-52	BALINESE⁶	• • •	JT · JT · JT
35-36	BIRMAN	• • •	JT,e · JT,c · JT,c
37-39	RAGDOLL	none	HW,d
82	Snowshoe	none	Ec
49	TURKISH VAN	• • •	JT · F• · JT · JT
70	TONKINESE	none	JT
65-67	BURMESE	none	WE
78	RUSSIAN BLUE	none	B
64	Chartreux	none	B
79	KORAT	none	B
87	Havana Brown	none	C

BREEDS FOOTNOTES:

1 includes Himalayan (including Kashmir)
2 in both shorthair and semi-longhair coats
3 includes Bombay and Burmilla (see p.115)
4 includes Foreign White and Havana (UK names)
5 includes Colorpoint Shorthair (US name)
6 includes Javanese (American)

a two forms: pewter (orange eyes) and shaded silver (green eyes).
b the tortie-tabbies do not occur in combination with white
c all varieties have white boots
d varieties with white are in two forms: white-booted & full bi-color
e amber-, blue- or odd-eyed varieties in each color

COLOR KEY

Col	W	A	B	C	D	E	F	G	H	J	K	L	M	N
Colour	white	black	blue	chocolate	lilac	red	cream	cinnamon	fawn	caramel	apricot			

Recognized varieties chart – pages 120/121

The chart on the previous page shows the range of varieties that are currently accepted for each breed. The situation is not static, however, for breeders are continually striving to increase the diversity and even create new breeds. The varieties represented in the chart (more than 2,500 overall) are, for the most part, those recognized by the CFA or, for those breeds not recognized in the USA, by the GCCF. The variety range shown for a breed recognized by both the CFA and the GCCF is the one accepted by the latter; in general the range accepted by the CFA for such breeds will be smaller.

The breeds are color-coded to section; e.g. semi-longhairs are green. The headed columns indicate the various coats that exist among cats. Letters in a box indicate the occurrence of that particular coat type in the breed concerned. A large capital letter denotes the color range in which the coat type can occur, as indicated in the small chart at the bottom. Where entries are present in a tabby column they can occur in whatever pattern type is indicated as acceptable in the block of small boxes immediately following the breed name. Thus the letter G in the tabby column (usual coat) for the Cymric breed indicates that black, blue, red and cream tabby varieties are recognized, which can be in either classic or mackerel patterns.

A small capital **T** next to a letter indicates that the tortoiseshell colors also occur within that pattern group; these will be in the same range of colors denoted by the letter but excluding, if present in the indicated range, red, cream and apricot.

A small capital **W** next to a letter indicates that the same range of colors in that pattern, including tortoiseshell when present, also occurs in combination with white, i.e. as bi-colors, tabby-and-white or tri-colors. Small lower case letters in the boxes relate to the footnotes above the color key.

Some of the shell and shaded boxes in the columns concerned with tipped coats are combined into a single box. In the breeds concerned no distinction is made between the two degrees of tipping, i.e. both are allowed within the one variety group standard. Where black (A) is the only indicated color in the standard shell/shaded column, the word "golden" forms part of the variety's name.

Glossary

Words in *italics* have their own entry (two such words together may have separate entries, not just one).

The British may use a different word from Americans to refer to the same thing; such words are indicated by (UK) or (US) after an entry word; this denotes the country in which the word is used, its alternative in the other country being given in the text that follows.

Some of the terms in this glossary are open to interpretation; because of this, or perhaps because of confusion or imprecise usage, some of them may be used with slightly different meanings in other books.

agouti – the fundamental coat pattern of many mammals, including cats, in which each *guard hair* has one or more pale yellow bands (the agouti bands) between darker bands (that can be any one of ten or so colors), giving the coat a flecked look (*ticking*); in domestic cats a *tabby* pattern of unbanded hairs (in the same color as the darker bands in the agouti hairs) is always superimposed on the agouti pattern; removal of the agouti band by the *non-agouti* gene gives rise to overall *solid* color (but this gene is ineffectual on red, cream and apricot).

awn hair – the longer and thicker of the two types of hair in a cat's *undercoat*; see also *guard hair* and *down hair*.

bi-color – describes a coat of any *solid* color with extensive white areas; sometimes used to refer to any coat with white areas.

blaze – a mark, often white, running down the face from the forehead.

blotched tabby – see *classic tabby*.

brindling – the occurrence of stray hairs of contrasting color (often white) in an otherwise uniform area of the coat.

calico (US) – *tortoiseshell* & white.

cameo – (US) a red- or cream- (dilute cameo) *tipped silver* variety in any breed; (UK) a red-, cream- or *tortie*-tipped silver variety of the *Persian type* Long Hair.

champagne (US) – chocolate (in Burmese and Tonkinese).

chestnut (US) – chocolate.

chinchilla – generically (esp. in US) a cat with a *shell tipped silver* coat; specifically (UK) the black shell tipped silver variety of the *Persian type* Long Hair.

chocolate (US) – sometimes chestnut; champagne (in Burmese and Tonkinese).

classic tabby – a *tabby* pattern of broad bands, forming an oyster mark on the flanks, a butterfly mark over the shoulders, longitudinal along the spine and broadly ringed around the legs and tail; also called blotched tabby.

cobby – of a compact, stocky body *type*, with a large rounded head, medium to short legs and a short tail, as seen in cats of *Persian type* and the British Shorthair; see also *foreign*.

colorpoint – a coat pattern in which the color/pattern is restricted to the *points*, the remainder of the body being a uniform, contrasting, paler color; also called (UK) Siamese pattern, or (US) Himalayan pattern; colorpointed cats generally have the word "point" in their name, prefixed by the color/pattern.

conformation – synonymous with *type*.

dilute – describes a color of a *self* or patterned cat influenced by the action of the dilution gene; thus blue is a dilute black, and blue-cream is dilute *tortoiseshell*.

double coat – a coat that includes an *undercoat*.

down hair – the shorter and softer of the two types of hair that make up a cat's *undercoat*; they are crimped and give the coat a woolly texture; see also *guard hair* and *awn hair*.

fancy – a collective term encompassing the organizations and individuals devoted to *pedigree* cats.

flame point (US) – red *point*; (see also *colorpoint*).

foreign (*type*) – describes cats tending towards the fine-boned, elegant body *type* shown to the extreme by Siamese, rather than the *cobby* Persian-type or British Shorthair type; see also *oriental*.

frost point (US) – lilac *point*; see also *colorpoint*.

golden – the name of the variety with black *shell* or *shaded tipping* on otherwise *standard* colored hairs in some breeds.

guard hair – the long, bristle-like hair that makes up the outer layer of the coat; see also *awn hair* and *down hair*.

Himalayan pattern (US) – *colorpoint*.

hock – the pointed angle at the top of the long ankle of the hind leg.

laces (US) – gauntlets, i.e. white markings extending in a narrow line from the foot up the back of the *hock*; seen particularly in Birman and Snowshoe breeds.

lavender (US) – lilac.

lilac (UK) – lavender; platinum (in Burmese and Tonkinese).

lynx point (US) – *tabby point*; see also *colorpoint*.

mackerel tabby – a *tabby* pattern of narrow stripes, vertical on the sides, longitudinal along the spine and ringed around the legs and tail.

mask – loosely the face, including the *muzzle* and ears.

mi-ke – the *calico* (tortoiseshell and white) variety of the Japanese Bobtail.

muzzle – nose and jaws, forward of the cheeks and including the whisker pads.

non-agouti – describes a coat or cat influenced by the non-*agouti* gene, which effectively converts the basic *tabby* pattern into an overall *solid* color (but this gene is ineffectual on red, cream and orange colors).

non-patterned *agouti* (mainly US) – *ticked tabby*.

nose leather – the bare nose tip, including the nostrils.

oriental (*type*) – often used as a synonym for *foreign* but usually implies an extreme of that *type* as exemplified by Siamese and Oriental Shorthairs.

pastel points – *shell* or *shaded tipped* varieties of the Siamese (experimental).

patched tabby (US) – *tortie-tabby*.

pedigree – the details of the ancestry of an individual member of a recognized breed or the document on which such details are recorded.

Persian *type* – describes cats with the extreme stocky, round-headed, *cobby* body *type* of the Persian (UK – Long Hair) and Exotic breeds; see also *foreign*.

pewter – a black-*tipped* form of *shaded silver* but with orange eyes, not green (in the Exotic and Persian breeds only).

platinum (US) – lilac (in Burmese and Tonkinese).

points – 1. the extremities (face, ears, tail lower legs and feet), contrastingly colored in Siamese and other *colorpointed* breeds; used in conjunction with a color, the word forms part of variety names within such a breed e.g., Blue Point Birman.
2. the individual features of a breed as described in its *standard*.

123

queen – a sexually mature female cat used for breeding.

registration – the recording of the existence of an individual cat and its *pedigree* by an official organization.

ruff – the longer fur around the neck of many cats.

scarab mark – an ornate M-shaped mark on the forehead of some spotted *tabbies* of *foreign type*, more complex than in other tabbies and fancifully likened to an ancient Egyptian scarab.

self/self-color – uniformly one color; also called (more descriptively but mainly in US) solid color.

sex-linked – describes a gene that is normally inherited differently by the two sexes e.g., the *tortoiseshell* pattern is usually restricted to females.

shaded – describes a coat (in an *agouti* cat) with medium length *tipping*; in the UK, however, the distinction between *tipped* (*shell*) and shaded is being phased out in some breeds and the latter term is then applied to both.

shadow points – *smoke* varieties of the Siamese (experimental).

shell – describes a coat (in an *agouti* cat) with short *tipping*; mainly an American term but used in this book as defined here to avoid confusion with its UK equivalent, *tipped*, which can have both a wider and a narrower meaning; see also *chinchilla*.

silver – a group designation applied to cats with colored *tipping* on otherwise white fur; if the term is not prefixed with another color e.g., blue silver, then specifically black tipping is implied; in silver *tabbies* the affected hairs are restricted to the paler areas between the darker markings; the word forms part of the variety name in tabbies but not necessarily in other variety groups that have tipped white fur.

single coat – a coat without an *undercoat*.

smoke – describes a *non-agouti* (*solid* or *tortie*) *coat* affected by the inhibitor gene, which turns only the base of the hairs white; the hairs, in effect, then bear colored *tipping* that is usually longer than that found in *shell* or *shaded* varieties.

solid – describes a single, unpatterned color.

solid-color (US) – *self-color*

spotted tabby – a *tabby* pattern of spots on the body, narrow markings on the legs and tail, and a *scarab mark* on the head.

standard – 1. a detailed description of a breed's features, or *points*, agreed by an official organization, representing the ideal against which animals are judged. 2. the normal colored, as distinct from *silver*, form of a *tipped* coat.

stop – a more or less pronounced angle in the nose/forehead profile.

tabby – a pattern of marks (blotches, stripes or spots) on a complementary,

paler, ground color in an *agouti* cat; named after "tabbi", a striped, silken cloth made in the Attabiya district of Baghdad; four tabby patterns occur *classic*, *mackerel*, *spotted* and *ticked*; see also *tortie-tabby*.

ticked tabby – a *tabby* pattern in which the stripes are restricted to markings on the head and sometimes faintly on the legs and tail; the remainder of the coat uniformly consists of *agouti* hairs; also called Abyssinian tabby and classically exemplified by the breed of that name; sometimes (mainly in US) misleadingly called non-patterned agouti.

ticking – the flecked effect seen in the areas between the markings in *tabby* coats that is created by the darker bands on *agouti* hairs.

tipped – describes a coat with *tipping*; used in the UK as part of the variety group name of some *silver* cats with specifically short (*shell*) tipping (but see *shaded*).

tipping – a contrasting, darker color at the tip of otherwise paler (giving *standard* varieties) or white (giving *silver* varieties) hairs; two lengths of colored tips are recognized in this book: short, which gives *shell* (UK – *tipped*) varieties in agouti cats only, and medium/long, which gives *shaded* varieties in agouti cats or *smoke* varieties in non-agouti cats; see also *golden* and *chinchilla*.

torbie – see *tortie-tabby*.

tortie – *tortoiseshell*.

tortie-tabby – a coat of any *tabby* pattern with any of the *tortoiseshell* colors superimposed upon it; also called (US) torbie or patched tabby.

tortoiseshell – a coat color arrangement consisting of more or less distinct interspersed patches of a *solid* color and red, cream or apricot; color pairings include: black, chocolate or cinnamon with red; blue, lilac or fawn with cream; or caramel with apricot; when not qualified with a color in a variety's name, specifically black/red is implied; depending on the size of the darker areas the underlying *tabby* pattern in the red, cream or apricot areas may be evident.

tri-color – describes a coat of any of the *tortoiseshell* colors with white.

type – the combined head and body features (mainly shape and size) that characterize a particular breed or breed group (see also *Persian type*, *foreign type* and *oriental type*).

undercoat – consists of *awn hairs* and *down hairs* and give the coat "body"; its degree of development varies between breeds; the undercoat hairs are mixed with but overlain by the longer, stiffer *guard hairs* that form the top coat.

van pattern – a *bi-color* coat pattern in which white predominates, the color being restricted to the head (between the ears and eyes) and the tail (which is faintly ringed)

Index

Page numbers in bold type refer to the breed's main entry or entries. Page numbers in medium type relate to mentions in another breed's text; some of these references may be useful when searching for similar looking cats. Numbers in parentheses refer to the number of a paw-note on the page concerned. The breeds are indexed here by both their American and British names, where applicable. Alternative and obselete names are also included.

TYPES (p.12)

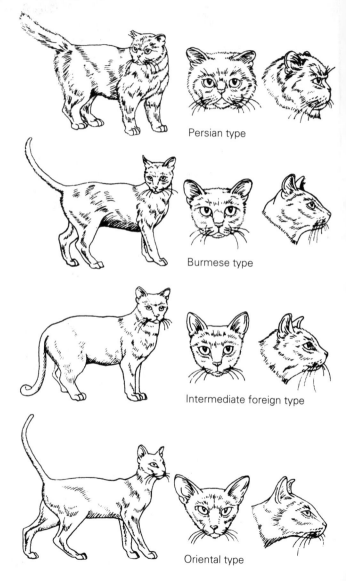

Persian type

Burmese type

Intermediate foreign type

Oriental type